Listening

T0324441

Listening

JEAN-LUC NANCY

TRANSLATED BY CHARLOTTE MANDELL

FORDHAM UNIVERSITY PRESS ✦ *New York*

This work was originally published in French as Jean-Luc Nancy, *À l'écoute* © 2002, Éditions Galilée, Paris. The two final essays, "How Music Listens to Itself" and "March in Spirit in Our Ranks," have been added by the author for the English-language edition.

Copyright © 2007 Fordham University Press

All rights reserved. No part of this publication may be reproduced, stored in a retrieval system, or transmitted in any form or by any means—electronic, mechanical, photocopy, recording, or any other—except for brief quotations in printed reviews, without the prior permission of the publisher.

Library of Congress Cataloging-in-Puplication Data

Nancy, Jean-Luc.
[A l'écoute. English]
Listening / Jean-Luc Nancy ; translated by Charlotte Mandell.—1st ed.
    p. cm.
Includes bibliographical references.
ISBN-13: 978-0-8232-2772-3 (cloth : alk. paper)
ISBN-10: 0-8232-2774-X (cloth : alk. paper)
ISBN-13: 978-0-8232-2773-0 (pbk. : alk. paper)
ISBN-10: 0-8232-2773-1 (pbk. : alk. paper)
1. Listening (Philosophy)   I. Mandell, Charlotte.   II. Title.
B105.L54N3613   2007
128'.4—dc22
                                                        2007009589

18 17 16   10 9 8 7 6
First edition

Listening

This is at the same time a title,
an address,
and a dedication.

The sound filled out that solitude to which the tone
gave rhythm ahead of time.
    —Raymond Queneau, *A Hard Winter*

Contents

Translator's Note ✦ *xi*

Listening ✦ *1*
  Interlude: Mute Music ✦ *23*
  Coda ✦ *45*

"March in Spirit in Our Ranks" ✦ *49*

How Music Listens to Itself ✦ *63*

Notes ✦ *69*

Translator's Note

Jean-Luc Nancy is a rewarding and demanding thinker. He is also exceptionally playful, witty, alert to the shapes and sounds of his words. The translator plods along behind the author's leaps, trying at least to explain what can't quite be caught on the wing. The translator's task is made all the more difficult by the way the semantic ranges of certain French words differ widely from their nominal English equivalents. And it is just such words that Nancy plays on here, plays with, delighting in the shimmer of their connotations.

Four words in particular should be kept in mind: *entendre* means both to hear and to understand. *Matrice* means both womb and matrix. *Renvoi* has an even wider range: return (as in return to sender, return a gift), send back (a parcel), repeat (a phrase or passage in music), refrain, refer, allude back . . . Our fourth word will demand most attention: *sens*. *Sens* means meaning, and it means sense—in all the meanings of that word in English, as in the senses five, feeling, intuition—as well as direction. I have tried to surmise the correct English choice in any given context, but the bracketed original will warn the reader of possible ranges. Add to these problems the fact that Nancy will often be using these and other words both in their "ordinary" meanings and in their special acceptations in musical discourse.

The music explicitly cited—from Wagner's *Tristan und Isolde*—at the end of the book is itself a sort of *renvoi*, sending the reader back to reread Jean-Luc Nancy's book as discourse not just upon language arts but upon tone arts too. So the reader is asked to keep an ear out for the possibilities—what you hear might be music.

Charlotte Mandell
Annandale-on-Hudson, NY
September 2006

Listening

*A*ssuming that there is still sense in asking questions about the limits, or about some limits, of philosophy (assuming, then, that a fundamental rhythm of illimitation and limitation does not comprise the permanent pace of philosophy itself, with a variable cadence, which might today be accelerated), we will ponder this: Is listening something of which philosophy is capable? Or—we'll insist a little, despite everything, at the risk of exaggerating the point—hasn't philosophy superimposed upon listening, beforehand and of necessity, or else substituted for listening, something else that might be more on the order of *understanding*?[1]

Isn't the philosopher someone who always hears[2] (and who hears everything), but who cannot listen, or who, more precisely, neutralizes listening within himself, so that he can philosophize?

Not, however, without finding himself immediately given over to the slight, keen indecision that grates, rings out, or shouts between "listening" and "understanding": between two kinds of hearing, between two paces [*allures*] of the *same* (the same *sense*, but what sense precisely? that's another question), between a tension and a balance, or else, if you prefer, between a sense (that one listens to) and a truth (that one understands), although the one cannot, in the long run, do without the other?

It would be quite a different matter between the view or the vision and the gaze, the goal or contemplation of the philosopher: figure and idea, theater and theory, spectacle and speculation suit each other better, superimpose themselves on each other, even can be substituted for each other with more affinity than the audible and the intelligible, or the sonorous and the logical. There is, at least potentially, more isomorphism between the visual and the conceptual, even if only by virtue of the fact that the *morphē*, the "form" implied in the idea of "isomorphism," is immediately thought or grasped on the visual plane. The sonorous, on the other hand, outweighs form. It does not dissolve it, but rather enlarges it; it gives it an amplitude, a density, and a vibration or an undulation whose outline never does anything but approach. The visual persists until its disappearance; the sonorous appears and fades away into its permanence.

What is the reason for this difference, and how is it possible? Why and how can there be one or several difference(s) of "senses" in general, and also difference(s) between the perceiving senses and the perceived meaning, "sensed sense" [*les sens sensibles et le sens sensé*]? Why and how is it that something of perceived meaning has privileged a model, a support, or a referent in visual presence rather than in acoustic penetration? Why, for example, does *acousmatics*, or the teaching model by which the teacher remains hidden from the disciple who listens to him, belong to a prephilosophical Pythagorean esoterism, just as, much later, *auricular* confession corresponds to a secret intimacy of sin and forgiveness? Why, in the case of the ear, is there withdrawal and turning inward, a making *resonant*, but, in the case of the eye, there is manifestation and display, a making *evident*? Why, however, does each of these facets also touch the other, and by *touching*, put into play the whole system of the senses? And how, in turn, does it touch perceived meaning? How does it come to engender it or modulate it, determine it or disperse it? All these questions inevitably come to the forefront when it's a question of listening.

Here we want to *prick up the philosophical ear*: to tug the philosopher's ear in order to draw it toward what has always solicited or represented philosophical knowledge less than what presents itself to view—form, idea, painting, representation, aspect, phenomenon, composition—but arises instead in accent, tone, timbre, resonance, and sound. We'll add another question as a temporary marker, to indicate the trembling discrepancy and dissymmetry of the two sides while still beginning to draw, to lure the ear (but also the eye along with it): Although it seems simple enough to evoke a *form*—even a *vision*—that is *sonorous*, under what conditions, by contrast, can one talk about a *visual sound*?

Or else: If, from Kant to Heidegger, the major concern of philosophy has been found in the appearance or manifestation of being, in a "phenomenology," the ultimate truth of the phenomenon (as something that appears as precisely distinct as possible from everything that has already appeared and, consequently, too, as something that disappears), shouldn't truth "itself," as transitivity and incessant transition of a continual coming and going, be listened to rather than seen? But isn't it also in the way that it stops being "itself" and identifiable, and becomes no longer the naked figure emerging from the cistern but the resonance of that cistern—or, if it were possible to express it thus, the echo of the naked figure in the open depths?

"To be all ears" [*être à l'écoute*, to be listening] today forms an expression that belongs to a register of philanthropic oversensitivity, where condescension resounds alongside good intentions; thus it often has a pious ring to it. Hence, for example, the set phrases "to be in tune with the young, with the neighborhood, with the world," and so on. But here I want to understand it in other registers, in completely different tonalities, and first of all in an ontological tonality: What does it mean for a being to be immersed entirely in listening, formed by listening or in listening, listening with all his being?

There is no better way to do this than to look beyond present usages. After it had designated a person who listens (who spies), the word *écoute* came to designate a place where one could listen in secret. *Être aux écoutes*, "to listen in, to eavesdrop," consisted first in being in a concealed place where you could surprise a conversation or a confession. *Être à l'écoute*, "to be tuned in, to be listening," was in the vocabulary of military espionage before it returned, through broadcasting, to the public space, while still remaining, in the context of the telephone, an affair of confidences or stolen secrets. So one aspect of my question will be: What secret is at stake when one truly *listens*, that is, when one tries to capture or surprise the sonority rather than the message? What secret is yielded—hence also made public—when we listen to a voice, an instrument, or a sound just for itself? And the other, indissociable aspect will be: What does *to be* listening, *to be* all ears, as one would say "to be in the world," mean? What does it mean to exist according to listening, for it and through it, what part of experience and truth is put into play? What is at play in listening, what resonates in it, what is the tone of listening or its timbre? Is even listening itself sonorous?

The conditions of this double interrogation refer first of all simply to the meaning of the verb *écouter*, "to listen." Consequently, to that kernel of meaning where the use of a sensory organ (hearing, the ear, *auris*, a word that gives the first part of the verb *auscultare*, "to lend an ear," "to listen attentively," from which *écouter*, "to listen," comes) and a tension, an intention, and an attention, which the second part of the term marks, are combined.[3] To listen is *tendre l'oreille*—literally, to stretch the ear—an expression that evokes a singular mobility, among the sensory apparatuses, of the pinna of the ear[4]—it is an intensification and a concern, a curiosity or an anxiety.

Every sensory register thus bears with it both its simple nature and its tense, attentive, or anxious state: seeing and looking, smelling and sniffing or scenting, tasting and savoring, touching and feeling or palpating, hearing and listening.

This last pair, however, the auditive pair, has a special relationship with *sense* in the intellectual or intelligible acceptance of the word (with "perceived meaning" [*sens* sensé], if you like, as opposed to "perceiving sense" [*sens sensible*]). *Entendre*, "to hear," also means *comprendre*, "to understand,"[5] as if "hearing" were above all "hearing say" (rather than "hearing sound"), or rather, as if in all "hearing" there had to be a "hearing say," regardless of whether the sound perceived was a word or not. But even that might be reversible: in all saying (and I mean in all discourse, in the whole chain of meaning) there is hearing, and in hearing itself, at the very bottom of it, a listening. Which means: perhaps it is necessary that sense not be content to make sense (or to be *logos*), but that it want also to resound. My whole proposal will revolve around such a fundamental resonance, even around a resonance as a foundation, as a first or last profundity of "sense" itself (or of truth).

If "to hear" is to understand the sense (either in the so-called figurative sense, or in the so-called proper sense: to hear a siren, a bird, or a drum is already each time to understand at least the rough outline of a situation, a context if not a text), to listen is to be straining toward a possible meaning, and consequently one that is not immediately accessible.[6]

We listen to someone who is giving a speech we want to understand, or else we listen to what can arise from silence and provide a signal or a sign, or else we listen to what is called "music."[7] In the case of these first two examples, one can say, at least to simplify (if you forget voices, timbres), that listening strains toward a present sense beyond sound. In the latter case, that of music, it is from sound itself that sense is offered to auscultation. In one case, sound has a propensity to disappear; in the other case, sense has a propensity to become sound. But here there are only two tendencies, precisely, and listening aims at—or is aroused by—the one where sound and sense mix together and resonate in each other, or through each other. (Which signifies that—and here again, in a tendential way—if, on the one hand, sense is sought in sound, on the other hand, sound, resonance, is also looked for in sense.)

When he was six years old, Stravinsky listened to a mute peasant who produced unusual sounds with his arms, which the future musician tried to reproduce: he was looking for a different voice, one more or less vocal than the one that comes from the mouth; another sound for another sense than the one that is spoken. A meaning with frontiers or one on the fringes of meaning, to paraphrase Charles Rosen.[8] To be listening is always to be on the edge of meaning, or in an edgy meaning of extremity, and as if the sound were precisely nothing else than this edge, this fringe, this margin—at least the sound that is musically listened to, that is gathered and scrutinized for itself, not, however, as an acoustic phenomenon (or not merely as one) but as a resonant meaning, a meaning whose *sense* is supposed to be found in resonance, and only in resonance.[9]

But what can be the shared space of meaning and sound? Meaning consists in a reference [*renvoi*]. In fact, it is made of a totality of referrals: from a sign to a thing, from a state of things to a quality, from a subject to another subject or to itself, all simultaneously. Sound is also made of referrals: it spreads in space,[10] where it resounds while still resounding "in me," as we say (we will return to this "inside" of the subject; we will return to nothing but that).

In the external or internal space, it resounds, that is, it re-emits itself while still actually "sounding," which is already "re-sounding" since that's nothing else but referring back to itself. To sound is to vibrate in itself or by itself: it is not only, for the sonorous body,[11] to emit a sound, but it is also to stretch out, to carry itself and be resolved into vibrations that both return it to itself and place it outside itself.[12]

Indeed, as we have known since Aristotle, sensing [*sentir*] (*aisthesis*) is always a perception [*ressentir*], that is, a feeling-oneself-feel [*se-sentir-sentir*]: or, if you prefer, sensing is a subject, or it does not sense. But it is perhaps in the sonorous register that this reflected structure is most obviously manifest,[13] and in any case offers itself as open structure, spaced and spacing (resonance chamber, acoustic space,[14] the distancing of a repeat [*renvoi*]), at the same time as an intersection, mixture, covering up in the referral [*renvoi*] of the perceptible with the perceived as well as with the other senses.

One can say, then, at least, that meaning and sound share the space of a referral, in which at the same time they refer to each other, and that, in a very general way, this space can be defined as the space of a *self*, a subject. A *self* is nothing other than a form or function of referral: a *self* is made of a relationship *to* self, or of a presence *to* self, which is nothing other than the mutual referral between a perceptible individuation and an intelligible identity (not just the individual in the current sense of the word, but in him the singular occurrences of a state, a tension, or, precisely, a "sense")—this referral itself would have to be infinite, and the point or occurrence of a *subject* in the substantial sense would have never taken place except in the referral, thus in spacing and resonance, at the very most as the dimensionless point of the *re-* of this resonance: the repetition where the sound is amplified and spreads, as well as the turning back [*rebroussement*] where the echo is made by making itself heard. A subject *feels:*[15] that is his characteristic and his definition. This means that he hears (himself), sees (himself), touches (himself), tastes (himself), and so on, and that he thinks himself or represents himself, approaches himself and strays from himself, and thus always feels himself feeling a "self" that escapes [*s'échappe*] or hides [*se retranche*] as long as it resounds elsewhere as it does in itself, in a world and in the other.

To be listening will always, then, be to be straining toward or in an approach to the self (one should say, in a pathological manner, *a fit of self*: isn't [sonorous] sense first of all, every time, a *crisis of self*?).[16]

Approach to the self: neither to a proper self (I), nor to the self of an other, but to the form or structure of *self* as such, that is to say, to the form, structure, and movement of an infinite referral [*renvoi*], since it refers to something (itself) that is nothing outside of the referral. When one is listening, one is on the lookout for a subject, something (itself) that identifies *itself* by resonating from self to self, in itself and for itself, hence outside of itself, at once the same as and other than itself, one in the echo of the other, and this echo is like the very sound of its sense.[17] But the sound of sense is how it refers to *itself* or how it *sends back to itself* [s'envoie] or *addresses itself*, and thus how it makes sense.

But here it is a question of being on the watch [*être aux aguets*] for a way that is precisely not that of a *watch* [guet] in the sense of a visual surveillance.[18] The sonorous here makes clear its singularity in relation to the optical register, where the relationship to the intelligible as a *theoretical* relationship (*theoretical* is linked, in Greek, to seeing) is more manifestly, if we can use this word, in play.[19] In terms of the gaze, the subject is referred back to itself as object. In terms of listening, it is, in a way, to itself that the subject refers or refers back. Thus, in a certain way there is no relationship between the two. A writer notes: "I can hear what I see: a piano, or some leaves stirred by the wind. But I can never see what I hear. Between sight and hearing there is no reciprocity."[20] In the same way, I would say that music floats around painting much more than painting is outlined around music. Or, in semi-Lacanian terms, the visual is on the side of an imaginary capture (which does not imply that it is reduced to that), while the sonorous is on the side of a symbolic referral/*renvoi* (which does not imply that it exhausts its amplitude). In still other words, the visual is tendentially mimetic, and the sonorous tendentially methexic (that is, having to do with participation, sharing, or contagion), which does not mean that these tendencies do not intersect. A musician writes: "How is it that sound has such a particular impact, a capacity to affect us, which is like nothing else, and is very different from what has to do with the visual and with touch? It is a realm we still do not know."[21]

In these statements, which I adopt for my own, there is no doubt more empiricism than theoretical construction. But the challenge in a study of the senses and of perceptible qualities is necessarily the challenge of an empiricism by which one attempts a conversion of experience into an a priori condition of possibility . . . of the experience itself, while still running the risk of a cultural and individual relativism, if all the "senses" and all the "arts" do not always have the same distributions everywhere or the same qualities.

Still, what we are thus calling "relativism" in turn constitutes an empirical material that makes a condition of possibility for any "sensation" or for any "perception" as well as for any "culture": it is the referral of one to the other that makes both possible. The difference between cultures, the difference between the arts, and the difference between the senses are the conditions, and not the limitations, of experience in general, just as the mutual intricacy of these differences is, as well. Even more generally, one could say that *the difference in sense* (in the "perceived" [*sensé*] sense of the word) *is its condition, that is, the condition of its resonance*. But nothing is more remarkable, in this order of consideration and experience, than the history of music, more than any other artistic technique, in the course of the twentieth century: the internal transformations following Wagner, the increasing importations of references outside of music labeled "classical," the arrival of jazz and its transformations, then that of rock and all its variations up to their present hybridizations with "scholarly" music, and throughout all these phenomena the major transformation of instrumentation, down to the electronic and computer production of sounds and the remodeling of schemes of sonority (timbres, rhythms, notations) which itself is contemporaneous with the creation of a global sonorous space or scene whose extraordinarily mixed nature—popular and refined, religious and profane, old and recent, coming from all continents at once—all that has no real equivalent in other domains. A musical-becoming of sensibility and a global-becoming of musicality have occurred, whose historiality remains to be thought about, all the more so since it is contemporaneous with an expansion of the image whose extent does not correspond to equivalent transformations in the perceptible realm.

To be listening is thus to enter into tension and to be on the lookout for a relation to self: *not*, it should be emphasized, a relationship to "me" (the supposedly given subject), or to the "self" of the other (the speaker, the musician, also supposedly given, with his subjectivity), but to the *relationship in self*, so to speak, as it forms a "self" or a "to itself" in general, and if something like that ever does reach the end of its formation. Consequently, listening is passing over to the register of presence to self, it being understood that the "self" is precisely nothing available (substantial or subsistent) to which one can be "present," but precisely the resonance of a return [*renvoi*].[22] For this reason, listening—the opening stretched toward the register of the sonorous, then to its musical amplification and composition—can and must appear to us not as a metaphor for access to self, but as the reality of this access, a reality consequently indissociably "mine" and "other," "singular" and "plural," as much as it is "material" and "spiritual" and "signifying" and "a-signifying."[23]

This presence is thus not the position of a being-present: it is precisely not that. It is presence in the sense of an "in the presence of" that, itself, is not an "in view of" or a "vis-à-vis." It is an "in the presence of" that does not let itself be objectified or projected outward. That is why it is first of all presence in the sense of a *present* that is not a being (at least not in the intransitive, stable, consistent sense of the word),[24] but rather a *coming* and a *passing*, an *extending* and a *penetrating*. Sound essentially comes and expands, or is deferred and transferred. Its present is thus not the instant of philosophico-scientific time either, the point of no dimension, the strict negativity in which that mathematical time has always consisted. But sonorous time takes place immediately according to a completely different dimension, which is not that of simple succession (corollary of the negative instant). It is a present in waves on a swell, not in a point on a line; it is a time that opens up, that is hollowed out, that is enlarged or ramified, that envelops or separates, that becomes or is turned into a loop, that stretches out or contracts, and so on.

The sonorous present is the result of space-time: it spreads through space, or rather it opens a space that is its own, the very spreading out of its resonance, its expansion and its reverberation. This space is immediately omnidimensional and transversate through all spaces: the expansion of sound through obstacles, its property of penetration and ubiquity, has always been noted.[25]

Sound has no hidden face;[26] it is all in front, in back, and outside inside, *inside-out* in relation to the most general logic of presence as appearing, as phenomenality or as manifestation, and thus as the visible face of a presence subsisting in self. Something of the theoretical and intentional scheme tuned to optics vacillates around it. To listen is to enter that spatiality by which, *at the same time*, I am penetrated, for it opens up in me as well as around me, and from me as well as toward me: it opens me inside me as well as outside, and it is through such a double, quadruple, or sextuple opening that a "self" can take place.[27] To be listening is to be *at the same time* outside and inside, to be open *from* without and *from* within, hence from one to the other and from one in the other. Listening thus forms the perceptible singularity that bears in the most ostensive way the perceptible or sensitive (*aisthetic*) condition as such: the sharing of an inside/outside, division and participation, de-connection and contagion. "Here, time becomes space," is sung in Wagner's *Parsifal*.[28]

In this open and above all opening presence, in acoustic spreading and expansion, listening takes place *at the same time* as the sonorous event,[29] an arrangement that is clearly distinct from that of vision (for which, incidentally, there is no visual or luminous "event" either, in an entirely identical meaning of the word: visual presence is already there, available, before I see it, whereas sonorous presence *arrives*—it entails an *attack*, as musicians and acousticians say). And animal bodies, in general—the human body, in particular—are not constructed to interrupt at their leisure the sonorous arrival, as has often been noted. "The ears don't have eyelids" is an old theme that is often repeated.[30] Moreover, the sound that penetrates through the ear propagates throughout the entire body something of its effects, which could not be said to occur in the same way with the visual signal. And if we note also that "one who emits a

sound hears the sound he emits," one emphasizes that animal sonorous emission is necessarily also (here again, most
often) its own reception.

> A *sound* makes into a semi-presence the whole system of
> *sounds*—and that is what primitively distinguishes *sound*
> from *noise*. *Noise* gives ideas of the causes that produce
> it, dispositions of action, reflexes—but not a state of im-
> minence of an intrinsic family of sensations.[31]

In any case, as soon as it is present, the sonorous is omni-
present, and its presence is never a simple being-there or
how things stand, but is always at once an advance, penetration, insistence, obsession, or possession, as well as presence "on the rebound,"[32] in a return [*renvoi*] from one
element to the other, whether it be between the emitter
and the receptor or in one or the other, or, finally and
especially, between the sound and itself: in that between or
antrum [*entre ou antre*] of sound where it is what it is by
resounding according to the play of what acoustics distinguishes as its components (volume, length, intensity, attack,
harmonics, partials, long-distance noises, etc.) and whose
major characteristic is not to form merely the results of an
abstract decomposition of the concrete phenomenon, but
just as actually to *play* some against others *in* this phenomenon, in such a way that sound sounds or resounds always
beyond a simple opposition between consonance and dissonance, being made of an intimate harmony and dishar-
mony among its parts: being made, one should perhaps
end by saying, *of the discordant harmony that regulates the
intimate as such* . . . (And without forgetting, although

without being able to speak of it knowingly, the very singular role played in listening by what we call "acoustic oto-emissions" produced by the inner ear of the one who is listening: the oto- or self[*auto*]-produced sounds that come to mingle with received sounds, in order to receive them . . .)

All sonorous presence is thus made of a complex of returns [*renvois*] whose binding is the resonance or "sonance" of sound, an expression that one should hear—hear and listen to—as much from the side of sound itself, or of its emission, as from the side of its reception or its listening: it is precisely from one to the other that it "sounds." Whereas visible or tactile presence occurs in a motionless "at the same time," sonorous presence is an essentially mobile "at the same time," vibrating from the come-and-go between the source and the ear, through open space,[33] the presence of presence rather than pure presence. One might say: there is the *simultaneity* of the visible and the *contemporaneity* of the audible.

This presence is thus always within return and encounter. It *returns* (refers) to *itself*, it *encounters* itself or, better, occurs against itself, both in opposition to and next to itself. It is co-presence or, again, "presence in presence," if one can say that. But insofar as it does not consist in a being-present-there, in a stable, fixed being, yet is not elsewhere or absent, it is rather in the rebound of "there" or in its setting in motion, which makes it, the sonorous place ("sonorized," one is tempted to say, plugged into sound), a place-of-its-own-self, a place *as* relation to self, as the taking-place of a self, a vibrant place as the diapason of a subject or, better, as a diapason-subject. (The subject, a diapason? Each subject, a differently tuned diapason? Tuned to self—but without a known frequency?)

We should linger here for a long while on rhythm: it is nothing other than the time of time, the vibration of time itself in the stroke of a present that presents it by separating it from itself, freeing it from its simple *stanza* to make it into *scansion* (rise, raising of the foot that beats) and *cadence* (fall, passage into the pause). Thus, rhythm separates the succession of the linearity of the sequence or length of time: it bends time to give it to time itself, and it is in this way that it folds and unfolds a "self." If temporality is the dimension of the subject (ever since Saint Augustine, Kant, Husserl, and Heidegger), this is because it defines the subject as what separates *itself*, not only from the other or from the pure "there," but also from self: insofar as it waits for *itself* and retains *itself*, insofar as it desires (itself) and forgets (itself),[34] insofar as it retains, by repeating it, its own empty unity and its projected or . . . ejected [*projetée, ou . . . jetée*] unicity.[35]

So the sonorous place, space and place—and taking-place—*as* sonority, is not a place where the subject comes to make himself heard (like the concert hall or the studio into which the singer or instrumentalist enters); on the contrary, it is a place that becomes a subject insofar as sound resounds there (rather, mutatis mutandis, as the architectural configuration of a concert hall or a studio is engendered by the necessities and expectations of an acoustic aim). Perhaps we should thus understand the child who is born with his first cry as himself being—his being or his subjectivity—the sudden expansion of an echo chamber, a vault where what tears him away and what summons him resound at once, setting in vibration a column of air, of flesh, which sounds at its apertures: body and soul of some *one* new and unique. Someone who comes to himself by hearing him*self* cry (answering the other? calling him?), or sing, always each time, beneath each word, crying or singing, *exclaiming* as he did by coming into the world.

The setting in motion of place is identically that of the present instant. What subtracts the sonorous present from the negative and chronometric punctuality of the pure and simple present (time not folded, not beaten out, not modulated), is that this time of the successive addition of presents is *at the same time* the reprise of a present that is (already) past and reopening [*relance*] of a present (still) to come. It is in this sense that one can say, for example, "There is no physical time in music."[36]

One should recall here Husserl's whole analysis of time, but only in order to lead it to Gérard Granel's masterly treatment of it.[37] If I may be forgiven for grossly oversimplifying, I will recall only this: in order to describe awareness of time, Husserl uses the paradigm of listening to a melody.[38] He analyzes how the present of this perception is a present formed by the overlapping, in it or on it, of the present impression and the retention of the past impression, opening forward onto the impression to come. It is a present, consequently, that is not instantaneous, but differential in itself. Melody thus becomes the matrix of a thought of unity *of and in* diversity—even in divergence or in "divorcity" (separation in opposite directions [*sens*])—as much as of a diversity or divergence *of and in* unity. There is certainly no chance in the fact that music, and more precisely its listening, comes to support and expose a capture in principle [*une saisie principielle*] of unity in difference, and of the latter in the former. The unity of unity and the unity of difference, the unity of monitoring the melody and its modulation, its tune and its notes, if we can put it that way, is effectuated in what Husserl calls the "living present." This present is the *now* of a subject that gives, on first or final hearing [*instance*], its presence to the present, or its present to presence. In the terms I use here, I will say that the "living present" resounds, or that it is itself resonance and is only that: resonance of instances or stances of the instant, in each other.

Granel, however, raises his Heideggerian objection to this point: for this analysis, the difference was implicitly assigned as unity from which "the phenomenological gaze already causes to *bring out* [ressortir]"[39] *both* unity *and* diversity grasped or pronounced *as such*. Phenomenonological intentionality thus diverges from what it had nonetheless been aiming for: the original "retreat" of each trait, unity and diversity, which does not offer itself *as such* but, on the contrary, plunges into what Granel calls "the Tacit" or "the silent difference that bears fruit in anything perceived." This is not, for Granel, anything but the retreat, the fugitivity, and the modesty of being in its Heideggerian sense. And this sense—to add a word to Granel's text—is the transitive sense of the verb *to be*,[40] according to which being "is being [*est l'étant*]" in a transitive mode (which is, however, neither a "doing" nor any operation . . .): a sense, thus, that is impossible to hear/understand, an unsignifiable sense but one that, perhaps, lets itself . . . be listened to. Forgetful of this retreat from being, Husserl, according to Granel, perpetuates the "forgetting of being" in the Heideggerian sense, and this occurs to the very extent that he does not concentrate his ear on musical resonance but rather converts it ahead of time into the object of an intention that configures it. Sound (and/or sense) is what is not at first intended. It is not first "intentioned": on the contrary, sound is what places its subject, which has not preceded it with an aim, in tension, or under tension.

On this account, we should say—even if this goes beyond Granel's statement—that music (or even sound in general) is not exactly a phenomenon; that is to say, it does not stem from a logic of manifestation. It stems from a different logic, which would have to be called evocation, but in this precise sense: while manifestation brings presence to light, evocation summons (convokes, invokes) presence to itself. It does not establish it any more than it supposes it already established. It anticipates its arrival and remembers its departure, itself remaining suspended and straining between the two: time and sonority, sonority as time and as meaning.[41] Evocation: a call and, in the call, breath, exhalation, inspiration and expiration. In *appellare*, what comes first is not the idea of "naming," but that of a pressure, an impulsion.

According to Granel: from melody to the silence that declares it by silencing the unity of its unity and of its difference, such is the beyond-phenomenonological ascent—that is to say ontological, still in the sense that in this case being continuously differs from all being-here-and-now. Which does not just mean that it is always different, but that it does not stop differing this difference itself: it does not let the difference be identified between two identities, since it is as the *différant*, indifferent to identity and to difference.

I propose to paraphrase by saying that it is a question of going back to, or opening oneself up to, the resonance of being, or to being as resonance. "Silence" in fact must here be understood [*s'entendre*, heard] not as a privation but as an arrangement of resonance: a little—or even exactly . . .—as when in a perfect condition of silence you hear your own body resonate, your own breath, your heart and all its resounding cave.[42] It is a question, then, of going back from the phenomenological subject, an intentional line of sight, to a resonant subject, an intensive spacing of a rebound that does not end in any return to self without immediately relaunching, as an echo, a call to that same self. While the subject of the target is always already given, posed in itself to its *point of view*, the subject of listening is always still yet to come, spaced, traversed, and called by itself, *sounded* by itself, if I can allow myself all these plays on words, trivial though they are, that the French language suggests here.[43] Although Granel did not formally declare it, the step he wants to take, by so thoroughly working through the Husserlian description, from phenomenological order to ontological retreat and recoil, is not accidentally a step that goes from the gaze to listening: in a sense, it comes back to suggesting that Husserl persists in "seeing" the melody instead of listening to it . . .

The subject of the listening or the subject who is listening (but also the one who is "subject to listening" in the sense that one can be "subject to" unease, an ailment, or a crisis) is not a phenomenological subject. This means that he is not a philosophical subject, and, finally, he is perhaps no subject at all, except as the place of resonance, of its infinite tension and rebound, the amplitude of sonorous deployment and the slightness of its simultaneous redeployment—by which a voice is modulated in which the singular of a cry, a call, or a song vibrates by retreating from it (a "voice": we have to understand what sounds from a human throat without being language, which emerges from an animal gullet or from any kind of instrument, even from the wind in the branches: the rustling toward which we strain or lend an ear).[44]

Interlude: Mute Music

Taken at its word: *mot*, "word," from *mutum*, an emitted sound deprived of sense, the noise produced by forming *mu*.

Mutmut facere: to murmur, to mutter—*muzō*, to do *mu*, *mu*, to say *m*.

Not saying a word: just *m* or *mu*, *muttio*, *mugio*, to moo, *mûnjami*, *mojami*.

Muteness, *motus*, to become mute [*amuïr*], disappearance of a phoneme [*amuïssement*]: of the *t* at the end of the word *mot*.

Kindred sound: *mormurō*, *marmarah*, *murméti*, *murmeln*, murmur.

Falsely kindred root: *motus*, motion, movement of the lips, emotion.

Mumble, mutter, grumble, *mussitare* ["to grumble"; in its transitive form, to keep quiet about a thing], moan, whisper, grouch, grouse.

Between the lips, *mulla*, passage of the lips, *Mund*, *Maul*, mouth, mug [*gueule*].

Word for word, *muhen*, to form *muh*, meuh, moo.

Mund, mouth—*mucken*, *mokken*, mockery, *moquer*.

Münden, open up, lead to, pour out.

Muō, to close or keep silent, *mustēs*, *mustikos*, mystery (not to reveal).

Motet: poem or song.

Another kindred sound: *mouche* ["fly"], *musya*, *muia*, *musca*, *Mücke*.

Mmmmmmmm.

In Phoenician Ugarit, *Mot*, god of the harvest, dies on the threshing floor with the wheat, to be reborn at the next harvest. God of grain and of death.

. . . .

Mmmmmmm continues: repeats its murmuring, mouth closed, not even Om, the holy syllable opening the jewel in the lotus of meditation that empties itself of itself: not even the muted utterance in which Hegel heard the lack of articulation between vowel and consonant, like the defect of a night in which the cows are as black as from a blinding light, similar, yes, to the mooing of cows in the night, similar to the vagueness in which the concept loses its own differentiation, in which it wholly consists, similar, yes, to the furrow left in the air or on the paper by the withdrawal of the concept, by a vanishing of difference that does not produce identity, but the buzzing, the humming, the muttering and borborygmus of the consonant that only resounds, articulating no voice. Mmmmmmm resounds previous to the voice, inside the throat, scarcely grazing the lips from the back of the mouth, without any movement of the tongue, just a column of air pushed from the chest in the sonorous cavity, the cave of the mouth that does not speak. Not a voice, or writing, or a word, or a cry, but transcendental murmuring, the condition of all words and all silence, a primal or archiglottal sound in which I give my death rattle and wail, death agony and birth, I hum and growl, song, jouissance *and* souffrance, *motionless word, mummified word, monotone where the polyphony that rises from the bottom of the belly is resolved and amplified, a mystery of emotion, the substantial union of body and soul* [âme]*, body and* âmmmmm.

. . . .

We will thus have established that listening opens (itself) up to resonance and that resonance opens (itself) up to the self: that is to say both that it opens to self (to the resonant body, to its vibration) and that it opens to the self (to the being just as its being is put into play for itself). But being put into play [*une mise en jeu*], or the referral [*renvoi*] of a presence to something other than itself, or to an absence of thing, the referral of a *here* to an *elsewhere*, of a *given* to a *gift*, and always, in some respect, of *something* to *nothing* (to the *res* [thing] of *rien* [nothing])—that is called sense, or meaning [*le sens, ou du sens*].

Thus, the listener (if I can call him that) is straining to end in sense (rather than straining toward, intentionally), or else he is offered, exposed to sense. (In this respect, moreover, and to say it again, listening comes at the unity and disparity of sensorial dispositions sideways. It makes the perceptible registers and the intelligible register resound among themselves[1]—whether it be consonance or dissonance, symphony or *Klangfarbenmelodie*, even euphony or cacophony, or some other relationship of resolution or tension.)

Sense opens up in silence. But it is not a question of leading to silence as if to the mystery of the sonorous, as if to the ineffable sublimity that is always too quickly attributed to the musical in order to make an absolute sense heard there (at least according to a tradition born with romanticism—but certainly not foreign to the history of *sense* and of its truth in the West, if not elsewhere too). It is indeed a question, it must be a question till the end, of *listening to* this silence of meaning [*sens*]. This phrase is not a verbal evasion. Listening must be examined—itself auscultated—at the keenest or tightest point of its tension and its penetration. The ear is stretched [*tendue*] by or according to meaning—perhaps one should say that its tension is meaning already, or made of meaning, from the sounds and cries that signal danger or sex to the animal, onward to analytical listening, which is, after all, nothing but listening taking shape or function as being inclined toward affect and not just toward concept (which does not have to do with understanding [*entendre*]), as it can always play (or "analyze"), even in a conversation, in a classroom or a courtroom. Musical listening seems, then, to be like the permission, the elaboration, and the intensification of the keenest disposition of the "auditory sense." (Musical listening means, in the end, music itself, the music that, above all, *is listened to* [s'écoute], whether it is written down or not, and when it is written, from its composition all the way to its execution. It *is listened to* according to the different possible inflections of expression: it is made to be listened to, but it is first of all, in itself, the listening of self.)

This profound disposition—arranged, in fact, according to the profundity of a reverberation chamber that is nothing other than the body from end to end—is a relationship to meaning [*sens*], a tension toward it: but toward it completely ahead of signification, meaning in its nascent state, in the state of return [*renvoi*] for which the end of this return is not given (the concept, the idea, the information), and hence to the state of return without end, like an echo that continues on its own and that *is* nothing but this continuance going in a *decrescendo*, or even in *moriendo*.[2] To be listening is to be inclined toward the opening of meaning, hence to a slash, a cut in un-sensed [*in-sensée*] indifference at the same time as toward a reserve that is anterior and posterior to any signifying punctuation. In the spacing out of the opening [*entame*], the *attack* of sense resonates, and this expression is not a metaphor: the beginning of sense, its possibility and its send-off [*coup d'envoi*], its address, perhaps takes place nowhere but in a sonorous attack: a friction, the pinch or grate of something produced in the throat, a borborygmus, a crackle, a stridency where a weighty, murmuring matter breathes, opened into the division of its resonance. Once again, the birthing cry, the birth of the cry—call or complaint, song, rustling of self, until the last murmur.

Thus resounds, beyond a saying, a "meaning" [*vouloir-dire*, "meaning to say"] to which one must first give not the value of a will but the inchoate value of an articulatory or profferatory release that is still without intention and without vision of signification—since these are impossible without this release, which might resemble those impulses to speak when one has nothing actually to say—when making love, when suffering—or that might be "an enunciation without utterance," as Bernard Baas says in a commentary devoted to the "voice" according to Lacan.[3]

Following this commentary, we are once again led toward a radicalization of the "phenomenological voice" that Derrida recognizes in Husserl. Once again, moreover, and although in an entirely different vein from those of Derrida, Granel, or Lacoue-Labarthe, what is affected concerns the originarity [*originarité*], in the subject or, even better, as the subject of subject, of a difference: of a difference that is not content with dividing or differing the prime supposed unity (perfectly classic gesture ever since Kant), but that is nothing else, itself (in the identity, then, of the difference that it is: in the very midst of its discrepancy), but the return *to self* in which the self is supported, but is supported only in dehiscence or in differential *of self* (is supported, then, by faltering, lets itself be supported from outside).

Lacan calls the voice "the alterity of what is said": what, in the saying, is other than what is said,[4] in a sense the non-said or silence, but still the saying itself, and even that telling silence [*silence disant*] like the space in which "I hear myself" when I grasp significations, when I hear them coming from the other or from my thoughts (which is the same thing). I can hear them, in fact, only if I listen to them resound "in me." Alterity in relation to the "saying" of the "voice" so understood is thus in fact less that of a non-said than that of a non-saying in saying or of saying itself, where saying can resound, and thus properly say. Lacan writes: "The voice as distinct from sonorities . . . resounds,"[5] with which he wants to keep distinct speaking (signifying) sonorities.

But "pure resonance" (as Bernard Baas calls it) is still a sonority—or, if you prefer, an arch-sonority: thus it is not only, according to its "purity" (taken in a Kantian sense), a nonperceptible transcendental of signifying sonority but also, according to its "resonance" (which makes its nature), a "sonorous materiality, vibration that animates the auditory apparatus as much as the phonatory apparatus, or rather: that seizes all somatic locations where the phenomenal voice resonates (rhythmic pulsation, muscular contraction or relaxation, respiratory amplification, epidermal shiver . . . or everything we used to call, more or less confusedly, the manifestations of the 'speaking body [*corps parlant*].' "[6] Thus, transcendental resonance is also incorporated—even, strictly speaking, it is nothing but that incorporation (which it would be better to call: the opening up of a body). The possibility of sense is identified with the possibility of resonance, or of sonority itself. More precisely, the perceived possibility of sense (or, if you like, the transcendental condition of significance, without which it would have no meaning) is overlaid with the resonant possibility of sound: that is, when all is said and done, with the possibility of an echo or a return of sound to self in self.[7]

Sense is first of all the rebound of sound, a rebound that is coextensive with the whole folding/unfolding [*pli/dépli*] of presence and of the present that makes or opens the perceptible as such, and that opens in it the sonorous exponent: the vibrant spacing-out of a *sense* in whatever sense one understands or hears it. But this also signifies that sense consists first of all, not in a signifying intention but rather in a listening, where only resonance comes to resound (unless this listening is equally that of the resonance in self or that of someone listening for a sonorous source: in resonance, there is source and its reception . . .). Sense reaches me long before it leaves me, even though it reaches me only by leaving in the same movement. Or: there is only a "subject" (which always means, "subject of a sense") that resounds, responding to a momentum, a summons, a convocation of sense.

I would like to start from that and move a little further forward, going once again toward music, beyond abstract sonority.[8] For that, we should go resolutely to the end of what is implied, without letting ourselves be restrained by a primacy of language and signification that remains dependent on a whole onto-theological prevalence and even on what we can call a philosophical *anesthesia* or *apathy*.[9] To go to the end means, then, simultaneously:

—to treat "pure resonance" not only as the condition but as the very beginning and opening up of sense, as beyond-sense or sense that goes beyond signification;

—to treat the body, before any distinction of places and functions of resonance, as being, wholly (and "without organs"),[10] a resonance chamber or column of beyond-meaning (its "soul," as we say of the barrel of a cannon, or of the part of the violin that transmits vibrations between the sounding board and the back, or else of the little hole in the clarinet . . .);

—and from there, to envisage the "subject" as that part, in the body, that is listening or vibrates with listening to—or with the echo of—the beyond-meaning.

In a way, these three demands give the result of the preceding analysis. At the same time, they open up another question: we still have to wonder what we have just called "listening to the beyond-meaning [*l'écoute de l'outre-sens*]" consists in when we resolutely turn away from the signifying perspective as a final perspective. Which we have to do, if we want to be faithful not only to the rejection, evoked just now, of philosophizing anesthesia but especially to the demand that the twofold motive of listening and resonance carries. Yet this necessity, and this fidelity, do not present their petition to the philosopher alone: they present it just as much to anyone confronted with interpreting music, whether "interpretation" is taken in its hermeneutic or in its instrumental sense: since one is never exactly free of the other.

(*To play* music is to make it sound, and its sense is in its resonance [its composition is subjected to it, or destined to it]. But music itself, in order to be music, plays on the sonorous resources of bodies that are struck, rubbed, plucked, and it *plays them*. One can say of music that it silences sound and that it interprets sounds: makes them sound and make sense no longer as the sounds of something, but in their own resonance. Without any doubt, one can describe in similar terms what painting does with the colors of "nature," sculpture with matter and mass. But the descriptive terms—"interpretation," "play," "internal resonance"—are not drawn from music by chance, and do not have any exact counterparts in other registers. This can be carried to a higher power if one says that the musical interprets the mutual resonances of artistic and/or perceptible registers [Baudelaire's "correspondences"]. Or else, that if each register is able to interpret these resonances and the generality of resonance, it interprets itself musically every time: thus we can speak of mutual colorations or the friction of the arts or of the senses as modalities of a co-respondence whose paradigm remains sonorous . . .)

If *listening* is distinguished from *hearing* both as its opening (its attack) and as its intensified extremity, that is, reopening beyond comprehension (of sense) and beyond agreement or harmony (*harmony* [entente] or *resolution* in the musical sense), that necessarily signifies that listening is listening to something other than sense in its signifying sense.[11]

What it involves, then, is already well known with regard to musical listening, that is to say, also what we sometimes call musical meaning or its comprehension. The discourses already sustained around the possibility/impossibility of a musical *récit* [narration] and/or of a musical statement are countless, as well as around the relationship/nonrelationship between text and music in song. Countless, too, are the testimonies of an ever-renewed recourse, despite these discourses, to the vocabulary of narrative and expression to talk about listening to a piece of music.

I will take one single example, in the beautiful film by Jean-Louis Comolli and Francis Marmande, *Le Concert de Mozart*.[12] In it, we hear Michel Portal say of the Clarinet Concerto: "It tells about someone who is in love, and his grief at not being able to love"; or else we hear Francis Marmande ask: "What is the orchestra saying?" and Portal replies: "It is telling its stories, the clarinet is telling its own stories." Later he says again: "These are operas without words, they say what the words don't say." These statements can, of course, be thought of as being intended for a mass audience, but they are nonetheless spoken in a film that is obviously made for a select, music-loving or musical audience and, in any case, they are—as can easily be shown—scarcely exaggerated evidence of a perennial situation and difficulty in the discourse on music—at least so long as this discourse does not become, at the same time, an interrogation of its own conditions of possibility.[13] This kind of discourse purposefully mixes a register of metaphorical usage of a naïve attraction ("it tells about"—in every respect metaphors abound on the subject of music: for example, a full, throaty sound, *allegro*, chromaticism, *toccata*, etc.), simultaneously distanced as hyperbolic ("the stories of the clarinet") and a register that is in fact dialectic (to say the non-said and the unsayable).[14]

This mixture of registers in a kind of negative semantics or paradoxical hermeneutics of the musical does not amount to awkwardness. And it testifies to the fact that musical listening, in sonorities and in their rhythmic, melodic, and harmonic arrangements, *hears/understands* articulations and consecutions, sequences and punctuations. If semantics per se is absent (or seems to be identifiable only at the level of sentiment—love, complaint . . .),[15] the syntactic for its part, or else "phrasing," is not entirely so; far from it. Pierre Schaeffer writes: "The only possible introduction of language into music is that of conjunctions," encouraging us to spot all the but-or-and-hence-so-neither-since's throughout a musical piece.[16] The syntactic without semantics (or almost, as if conjunctions were not semantic . . .) would suggest a way of sampling the directional and sequential stratum of language, separate from all signification. This would no longer be language (if there is no longer the fundamental property of twofold articulation in morphemes and in phonemes),[17] but it would be, in language, something that belongs to it just as essentially as semantics, which is its diction (and which, moreover, plays some part in modulating or affecting the semantic). Sense, if there is any, when there is any, is never a neutral, colorless, or aphonic sense: even when written, it has a voice—and that is also the most contemporary meaning of the word *écrire* ["to write"], perhaps in music as well as in literature.[18] *Écrire* in its modern conception—elaborated since Proust, Adorno, and Benjamin, through Blanchot, Barthes, and to Derrida's *archi-écriture*—is nothing other than making sense resound beyond signification, or beyond itself. It is *vocalizing* a sense that, for classical thought, intended to remain deaf and mute, an understanding [*entente*] untimbred [*détimbrée*] of self in the silence of a *consonant* without resonance.

Francis Ponge writes: "Not only any poem at all, but any text at all—whatever it is—carries (in the full sense of the word), carries, I say, its speaking [*diction*]. / For my part—if I examine myself writing—I never come to write the slightest phrase without my writing being accompanied by a mental speaking and listening, and even, rather, without it being *preceded* by those things (although indeed just barely)."[19]

Speaking—speaking and listening, as Ponge makes clear, for speaking is already its own listening—is the echo of the text in which the text is made and written, opens up to its own sense as to the plurality of its possible senses. It is not, and in any case not only, what one can call in a superficial way the musicality of a text: it is more profoundly the music in it, or the arch-music of that resonance where it *listens to itself* [s'écoute], by listening to itself *finds itself* [se trouve], and by finding itself *deviates* [s'écarte] from itself in order to resound further away, listening to itself before hearing/understanding itself, and thus actually becoming its "subject," which is neither the same as nor other than the individual subject who writes the text.

To say is not always, or only, to speak, or else to speak is not only to signify, but it is also, always, to dictate, *dictare*,[20] that is, at once to give saying its *tone*, or its *style* (its tonality, its color, its allure) and for that or in that, in that operation or in that *tenseness* of saying, *reciting* it, reciting it *to oneself* or letting itself recite *itself* (make itself sonorous, de-claim itself or ex-claim itself, and cite itself (set itself in motion, call itself, according to the first meaning of the word, incite itself), send back to its own echo and, by doing so, make itself). Writing is also, very literally and even in the sense of an *archi-écriture*, a voice that resounds. (Here, no doubt, literary writing and musical writing touch each other in some way: from behind, so to speak. The question is then posed, for both, of listening to this voice as such, as it refers only to itself: that is to say, listening to what is not already encoded. Perhaps we never *listen* to anything but the non-coded, what is not yet framed in a system of signifying references, and we never *hear* [entend] anything but the already coded, which we decode.)[21]

In speaking [*diction*], starting with the speaking of a text, it is a question of two things together—and once again, of the unity and distinction of these two things: rhythm and timbre.

It is not that these two properties can be merely detached from their intricacy and from their involvement in melody and in harmony, and, with them, in all the canonical values of sound (pitch, intensity, duration, etc.). It is a question only of polarities, or of a twofold polarity where rhythm and timbre belong to each other and together come to the foreground of a musical universe from which other properties do not, indeed, disappear, but rather deconstruct a system where we see—or hear—"expression" and "diction" being disassembled.[22]

Rhythm and timbre—between them holding melodic and harmonic possibility—outline, in a way, the matrixlike constitution of resonance when it is placed in the condition of the phrasing or of the musical sense, that is to say, when it is offered to listening.[23] This condition is that of *diction* or "dictation" in general: de-clamation, ex-clamation, ac-clamation,[24] previous to music as well as to language, but common to them both while still dividing them, and at the same time the presence of each one of the two in the other: presence of sense as resonance, sonorous impulse, call, out-cry, address . . .

The womb[*matrice*]-like constitution of resonance, and the resonant constitution of the womb: What is the belly of a pregnant woman, if not the space or the antrum where a new instrument comes to resound, a new *organon*, which comes to fold in on itself, then to move, receiving from outside only sounds, which, when the day comes, it will begin to echo through its cry? But, more generally, more womblike, it is always in the belly that we—man or woman—end up listening, or start listening. The ear opens onto the sonorous cave that we then become.

In his analysis of rhythm, Lacoue-Labarthe shows how rhythm is argued in Plato, so as to be included in the mi-metic logic of a representation or an expression of the fig-ure, itself considered as a character or *ethos*. This logic is none other than that of diction: expression of a "behavior" or a mood (courage, for example, or supplication). There is no reason to go over this analysis, which refers step by step to all the mimetological hermeneutics of music (narra-tives, acting out of emotions, etc.). One might only suggest adding here: beyond the codes that have linked some senti-ment or other, *pathos* or *ethos*, to some musical mode or other (rhythm, tonality, etc.), it is the nonmusical codification of affects themselves that we should be interested in (what do we label love, desire, passion, joy, chagrin, bravura, etc.?), not without wondering, too, if it is possible to separate completely an order of affects from an order of musical *mimesis* that would follow, or if both are not interwoven into each other and by each other (in the cry, the complaint, the groan, in the sonorous emission as such, its opening, its ex-pression, its mouth open and its body shaken . . .). Even further, we would have to go so far as to touch a fundamental rhythmic of affect as such, namely—perhaps—the beat of a blending together and a pulling apart, of an accepting/rejecting or a swallowing/spitting:[25] in fact, from movement (impulse?) from which there comes an outside and an inside and, thus, something or someone like a "subject."

My aim does not extend to that. But I should point out that such a direction of the investigation would lead us toward the formation of a subject first of all as the rhythmic reployment/deployment of an enveloping between "inside" and "outside," or else folding the "outside" into the "inside,"[26] invaginating, forming a hollow, an echo chamber or column, a resonance chamber (well before any possibility of a visible figure presentable in reflection: long before any "specular identification"). The same direction would take us toward an aspect of rhythm different from the one that mimetic and "typographical"[27] logic arrests and freezes in place: namely, rhythm as figure "broached by time,"[28] hence moving and fluid, syncopated, beaten out as a measure is and, consequently, linked to dance (as, moreover, Benveniste indicates in his study of the word *rhusmos*). Rhythm not only as scansion (imposing form on the continuous) but also as an impulse (revival of the pursuit).[29]

But what is a figure that is throbbed as well as stressed, "broached by time," if not a figure that has already lost *itself* and that is still expecting *itself*, and that *calls to itself* (which cries out to self, which gives itself or receives a name)? What else is it but a subject—and then isn't the subject itself the starting of time in both values of the genitive: it opens it and it is opened by it? Isn't the subject the *attack of time?*

In the time of this attack, before sound per se, there is the friction of the thing beaten, between outside and inside, in the fold/unfold of the beginning of a dance: there is the release of a body, the spacing and mobile configuration of a subject, which comes down to saying, identically, the possibility and necessity of resonance. In other words, to the point where we now are: the timbre of the echo of the subject. Rhythm, dancing, opens up timbre, which re-sounds in the rhythmed space.

Actually, I never stop talking about timbre, and as a philosopher I seek to give timbre [*timbrer*] to my discourse.

Not in order to establish timbre in a primary or dominant position in relation to the other elements or components—as they are sometimes called—of music. Rather, to convey this: in speaking of timbre, one is aiming precisely at what does not stem from a decomposition: even if it remains possible and true to distinguish it from pitch, duration, intensity, there is, however, no pitch, and so on, without timbre (just as there is no line or surface without color). We are speaking, then, of the very resonance of the sonorous.

As Antoine Bonnet says, "timbre is the modern name for sound," and "timbre is the *reality* of music."[30] Timbre comes to us today—by virtue of the history of the contemporary mutation of music—as sonorous matter, and sonorous matter is precisely what, while still remaining matter (voluminous and impenetrable: in the present case, rather strongly penetrating), spreads out in itself and resounds in (or from) its own spacing. Timbre is thus the first correlative of listening, and it is through it that we can even better approach what is straying here from a simple phenomenology. Rather than speaking of timbre and listening in terms of "intentional aim," it is necessary to say that before any relationship to object, listening opens up in timbre, which resounds in it rather than for it.[31] In truth, resonance is at once listening to timbre and the timbre of listening, if one may put it that way. Resonance is at once that of a body that is sonorous for itself and resonance of sonority in a listening body that, itself, resounds as it listens. (At the same time, this resonance is not an immobile given, since timbre itself is an evolving process,[32] and, consequently, listening evolves along with it.)

Timbre is the resonance of sound: or sound itself. It forms the first consistency of sonorous *sense* as such, under the rhythmic condition that makes it resound (even a simple monotone sustained contains rhythm and timbre). *Sense*, here, is the ricochet, the repercussion, the reverberation: the echo in a given body, even *as* this given body, or even as the gift to *self* of this given body. That is why Wittgenstein, after discussing the borderline, or imaginary, experience of hearing a sound separated from its timbre, comes to take timbre as a privileged image of what he calls "private experience," consequently, experience that is not communicable.[33] I would say that timbre is communication of the incommunicable: provided it is understood that the incommunicable is nothing other, in a perfectly logical way, than communication itself, that thing by which a subject makes an echo—of self, of the other, it's all one—it's all one in the plural.

Communication is not transmission, but a sharing that becomes subject: sharing as subject of all "subjects." An unfolding, a dance, a resonance. Sound in general is first of all communication in this sense. At first it communicates nothing—except itself. At its weakest and least articulated degree, one would call it a noise. (There is noise in the attack and extinction of a sound, and there is always noise in sound itself.) But all noise also contains timbre. In a body that opens up and closes at the same time, that arranges itself and exposes itself with others, the noise of its sharing (with itself, with others) resounds: perhaps the cry in which the child is born, perhaps an even older resonance in the belly and from the belly of a mother.

Still, timbre is not a *single* datum. Its very characteristic is itself to be, more than a component, a composition whose complexity continues to increase as acoustic analysis is refined and as it goes beyond mere determination of a sound by its harmonics.[34] Timbre is above all the unity of a diversity that its unity does not reabsorb. That is also why it does not yield to measurement or notation as do the other musical values (which, however, can never be identified—even pitch—with strict mathematical values). Its very name differs from those that refer to measure, like "pitch," "duration," "intensity." Timbre opens, rather, immediately onto the metaphor[35] of other perceptible registers: color (*Klangfarbe*, "color of sound," the German name for timbre), touch (texture, roundness, coarseness), taste (bitter, sweet), even evocations of smells. In other words, timbre resounds with and in the totality of perceptible registers. In this resonance, the mutual *mimesis* of senses, if there is one, is not distinguished from the already evoked *methexis*: participation, contagion (contact), contamination, metonymic contiguity rather than metaphoric transference.[36]

As for the literal meaning of the word *timbre*, it comes from the Greek *tympanon*, that is, the tambourine of orgiastic cults and, before that, from the Semitic *top*, *tuppim*, also meaning tambourine.[37] Strike, dance and resonance, a setting in motion and start of an echo: the means by which a "subject" arrives—and leaves itself, absents itself from its own arrival. "Timbre, style, and signature are the same obliterating division of the proper [*propre*]," Derrida wrote.[38] How they are "the same," however, can only be approached as a resonance between them, or as a mutual "figuration" by metonymy.

Timbre can be represented as the resonance of a stretched skin (possibly sprinkled with alcohol, the way certain shamans do), and as the expansion of this resonance in the hollowed column of a drum. Isn't the space of the listening body, in turn, just such a hollow column over which a skin is stretched, but also from which the opening of a mouth can resume and revive resonance? A blow from outside, clamor from within, this sonorous, sonorized body undertakes a simultaneous listening to a "self" and to a "world" that are both in resonance. It becomes distressed (tightens) and it rejoices (dilates). It listens to itself becoming distressed and rejoicing, it enjoys and is distressed at this very listening where the distant resounds in the closest.

That being the case, that skin stretched over its own sonorous cavity, this belly that listens to itself and strays away in itself while listening to the world and while straying in all directions, that is not a "figure" for rhythmic timbre, but it is its very pace, it is my body beaten by its sense of body, what we used to call its soul.

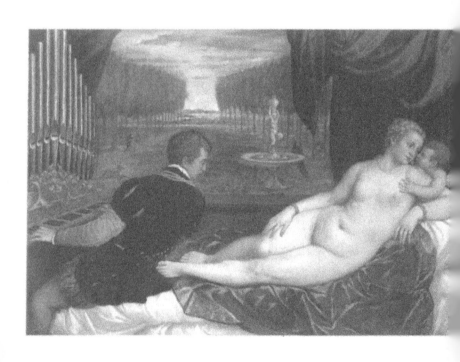

Coda

We'll add an image here, which has not been much commented on: Titian painted this Venus listening to an organ-player.[1] Evidently—it is clearly shown—the musician is gazing sensually at the woman. But isn't this belly that he is gazing at the very place where his music comes to resound, and isn't it also the resonance of his instrument he is listening to? In this reverberation, the inside and the outside open up to each other. The background of the scene is not that of a room, but a park whose trees prolong the organ pipes in a perspective that turns toward us like a large resonance chamber. The ear opens onto the belly, or the ear even opens up the belly, and the eye resounds here: the image distances its own visibility to the back of its perspective, in the distance from which music returns, resounding with desire, so as, with it, not to stop letting its harmonics resound.

From very far away, in the arts and in time, one can reply to this painting with music by Wagner, the instant that Tristan, to Isolde's voice, cries out: *What, am I hearing light?*—before he dies in front of the woman who will survive him only long enough to join him in the song of death that she is *alone in hearing*, in the breath of death that becomes *the melody that resounds* and that will mingle with, and resolve into, *the mass of waves, the thunder of noises, in the All breathing with the breath of the world.*

*"March in Spirit
in Our Ranks"*

*I*t would be useful, if not plausible, to imagine that if Nietzsche ended up preferring Bizet to Wagner, even if that was out of ironic provocation, it was because Bizet, in *Carmen*, put military music to the test of a joyful imitation (not even a parody) with the band of children chanting "avec la garde montante." Not a parody, and not a satire either, but a simple diversion into liveliness and play, in the bright clarity of children's voices, of the cadence of the procession, the parade, in a time when it was still possible to perceive the military march as a likeable ornament of garrison life, like a folkloric rite whose "march" quality referred to the perpetual back and forth of the sentries, who were devoted above all to guarding their ritual and the tradition of their own panache.

It was quite a different thing, of course [*bien entendu*] (here it is only a question of that, of *entendre* [hearing/ understanding] and of hearing well), in the musical marches that herald innocent Parsifal's approach to the Grail Hall. These had none of the quality of a playful back and forth, but rather of a sublime, literally endless procession in a place where time itself "becomes space" (as Gurnemanz says), that is, in a place where the future unfurls and is enacted in a realization that is itself destined to expand indefinitely and to feed on its own exaltation. Furthermore, it wasn't even a question of a "military march," but of the ceremonial of the Order of Knights: and it was in the spirit of an Order, beyond any Army, that Hitler conceived of his own troops.

Still, Bizet, just as he always arouses at least a slight embarrassment among almost all the commentators on Nietzsche, is not in the least comparable to Wagner in the history of contemporary music. Bruckner, Mahler, Strauss owe nothing of note to him. And we need not pause here over the various complex relationships that Verdi, Puccini, or Debussy may have had with Wagner. We do not want to suggest anything, absolutely nothing, other than this: not only did Nazism treat and mistreat in its way the musical art it found before it, as it did all kinds of art and cultural production in general; but Nazism also benefited from an encounter, which was not a chance one, with a certain musical disposition, just as it also benefited from a similar encounter with a certain new condition, often the most modern, of dance and of architecture.

This is one way of saying that Nazism did not come out of nothing, like a mushroom, that it did not descend without warning, like a kind of *diabolus ex machina*, whose mechanical artifice and superficiality it would be easy enough, in the end, to reveal. Without in any way wanting—I emphasize this, knowing, however, that this kind of interpretation is always reborn from its ashes—to retrace an obscure genealogy of Nazism, I cannot prevent myself from noticing, when it is a question of music and of National Socialism, that something had already been preparing itself for a long time—something that did not as such prefigure the Third Reich, but that offered it a choice space.

Music, dance, architecture: this trio could be characterized as a trio of the arts of expansion, giving this term its most generous, least hegemonic definition, without, however, refusing to see, or even worse, without repressing the awareness that expansion, the opening of a wide space of exaltation, of highlighting [*mise en évidence*] and dramatizing [*mise en scène*], always harbors the most formidable of ambiguities. But it harbors this resource most dangerously exactly when it presents itself as, and when it sets out to be, expansion—outpouring, overflowing, dilation and sublimation, the propagation of a subjectivity.

* * *

Subjectivity cannot spread or take root without being propagated and communicated. Territorial expansion is only a metaphor for the osmotic, epidemic, contagious impulse (think of the morbid attraction the Nazis had to the image of microbial infection as applied to "subhumans," indicative, in fact, of their impulse toward contagion and the inoculation of their own virulence) that comprises the first justification for all forms of agitation, riot, and violence. In this example, "conquest" transforms its schema in a radical way: mastery of a territory (one that is relatively indifferent to the capture of souls), and even the submission and domination of populations, are followed by the capture and penetration of identities. Capture [*prise*] gives way to control [*emprise*], absorption to administration, penetration to simple jurisdiction.

Music harbors a force of communication and participation that all forms of secular, religious, or aesthetic power that have succeeded each other through our history have not failed to recognize since at least the time when the term *mousikē* designated the ensemble of forms and exercises of expression of a wider sense than the single sense signified by words. This expressive, communicative, pulse-shaping, disseminating power had acquired an entirely new consideration in the age of subjectivity, that is, in the age when every reference necessarily became a return to self and in self, the service of self to an entity essentially endowed with the power of self-reference: subject, conscience, identity, people, mind, living body, embodied force, will in action. From Schopenhauer to Nietzsche and Liszt to all the great mutants of music of the twentieth century, not only has the entire movement of thought been turned toward music as toward its own sublimity—toward its *metaphysics*, as Schopenhauer said—but one could assert that all the arts had projected into musical interiority and expressivity the need for an energy detached from the

moorings that till then had held fixed in place the con-
nected registers of cosmological structure (of harmonic
order) and of representational technique (of objective
reference).

The passage from a plastic and poetic paradigm to a
musical paradigm corresponds to this: the order of significations articulated according to the translation of an easily
identifiable and (re)constructible reality gives way to the
expressive order of an essentially ineffable intimacy (Schopenhauer called it "will"; the "will-to-live," that is to say,
being as desire rather than being as reason). That it was
not by chance that this change of paradigm accompanied a
change of world whose limits were sensed in advance by
Reason and the Enlightenment is beyond argument. Moreover, we still haven't emerged from the ways or wander-
ings that this change opened up. That fascism and Nazism
might have arisen out of it should not, though, make us
come to any conclusion about mechanical causality. But
that fascism and Nazism could, at the very least, arise from
it—that is also beyond argument. Among many other
things, the connecting thread of music in the history of
European thought keeps us from being satisfied with talking about "monstrosity" and about some deviation pure
and simple.

It is not necessary to repeat what is well known about
the powers and effects of music: whether we consider them
from psychological, sociological, or symbolic points of
view, their history is as ancient as the West, and Plato bears
witness to this when he sets out carefully to regulate the

modalities and uses of the musical art. It is necessary, rather, not to equivocate about the recognition of this fact: the resources of music (and of dance and architecture) in its capacities of harnessing, mobilization, and exaltation were not invented by the Nazis; people before them had already taken hold of those capacities, in the name of State, Church, or "worldview." We have not forgotten that it was not by chance that the division of the Christian community at the Reformation—a division that so strongly affected Germany—and the wars that followed it had a very marked musical translation, in Luther as well as in the Counter-Reformation. It is not excessive to state that this aspect of history belongs inseparably to religion and to music. Which means, by implication: to politics and to philosophy.

*   *   *

All that, in fact, is well known, and would not deserve to be recalled, if not for two purposes.

The first aim consists in insisting, stubbornly, on the intrinsic membership of fascisms (in general, of totalitarianisms) in the history of Europe and consequently in its essence or its truth. We must insist on this because this belonging is continually denied or at least made secondary in general, politically conformist consciousness. "Belonging," here, does not have to do with identity: but this word should at least serve as a warning signal that forbids us to be content with the thesis of demonic accident, as I mentioned above. To try to say it in few words: the National

Socialist tonality of music, from the "Horst-Wessel Lied" beaten out in cadence in the streets up to the "Ode to Joy" performed (no less in cadence) in a factory for combat tanks, is not purely foreign to the musical possibilities awakened long before Nazism (as much on the level of musical metaphysics and mythologies as on the level of modes of composition, of melodic and harmonic models, of timbres themselves and of orchestration). The connection, or continuity, stems from the idea of a music received as a summons to the most profound and ineffable interiority, to "sentiment" itself understood as collective and unique to a defined community, or rather, defined by being experienced in its own song (the "German song" that Hölderlin spoke of, especially the choral song that Brahms had illustrated so well, in close proximity to popular themes).

The second aim, though, consists in considering what, throughout this continuity, also represents the turning point of a shift or of a specific perversion. It is perhaps possible to characterize it this way: in that place where, in immediately previous history, the musical had become the privileged expression of a given "sentiment" or "soul," hidden in the deepest heart of the world, of humanity or even of a people, and thus the *katharsis* par excellence of a proof of being or of life (a feeling-oneself-live, suffer, enjoy, desire), in that place henceforth the relationship of the "given" and of the "experienced" was reversed. It was no longer a question so much of letting a fundamental affect come to expression but of shaping such an affect, of forming it and conforming it to a measure not yet registered in nature or in history (or merely registered in the form of an age-old archaicness, so remote that only myth could reach it).[1] Thus an inversion of sense was produced: the intimate and ineffable experience must give itself, re-create for itself, and forge for itself, its tonality, its voice, its sonority—insofar as, following the continuity, it is in sonority that it can and must pour out and be exalted in all its amplitude.

Goebbels said in 1937: "Art is nothing other than what shapes feeling. It comes from feeling and not from intelligence. The artist is nothing but one who gives direction [*sens*] to this feeling."[2] The artist, then, is only a relay between informal feeling and trained feeling endowed with meaning [*sens*]. It is implied, then, that sentiment needs to be given form and thus provided with a direction. If music best conveys collective sentiment—whether in the cosmic register or in that of belonging to some sort of community (of course, here we would have to elaborate on the appearance and flourishing of communitarian desire, in the same period as the one in which music and literature had been transformed)—then music must give direction [*sens*] to collectivity. Yet it will be less a question of going from a given community to its own song than of coming from it by means of song to a community thus formed. Feeling, which is at the source, must be captured and collected in order to take shape and meaning in an outpouring whose mode, tone, and regulation the artist masters, while himself following a precise purpose.

In a certain way, the operation passes through music (or any art) and over it: the "direction" that "forms" it is added to it as a finality that music itself does not have. The ineffable is charged with speaking. To remain on the level of words, one could say that the unspecified *Freunde* (friends) of Beethoven/Schiller [in the "Ode to Joy"] receive their configuration as *Volksgenosse* (ethnic or racial companions). And similarly, one could say that the Ninth Symphony derives its meaning—*salva musica*, in short, although the performance or interpretation is not immaterial—from the fact of being played in a Panzer factory, in the presence of valiant workers who are forming those modern images of Teutonic knighthood. And then again, one would have to say, despite some additional complications that I will set aside, that *The Ring Cycle* and *Parsifal* receive their meaning from the fact of being represented in the context of and according to the spirit of the Reich.

*   *   *

What truly betrays music and diverts or perverts the movement of its modern history is the extent to which it is indexed to a mode of signification and not to a mode of sensibility. Or else the extent to which a signification overlays and captures a sensibility. Then resonance—and dissonance—in an interminable and unfigurable law that had given music and/or its representation, ever since Schopenhauer and Beethoven (if we may link the two), its new vitality is found to be transposed (I don't dare say "transfigured," but "disfigured" might be fitting) into a signifying imposition that, in order to come to an end, can allow nothing to be resonant or dissonant, since there is no more room for anything but utterance and persuasion of a *sense* through a *form* supposed to constitute the adequate expression of this sense itself regarded as *content*. Thus *feeling* manages to be identified all at once as signified and signifier of realities, images, or concepts like "people," "community," "destiny," "mission," and so on.

Still, we should not be content rashly to impute solely to Nazism this return to a signifying order. Of course, the earlier history of music should itself be regarded from this viewpoint (as well as, for example, from the angle of what the various forms of "program music" have represented), with a precise and discriminating attention. But the fact remains that, in a massive way—and here that is a fitting expression—signifying and oversignifying imposition characterizes Nazi music. The same is true for dance and architecture, once again, but also for poetry as much as for the totality of forms of daily life, public and private: all specificity has a tendency to disappear in this imposition. Which is another way of saying that Nazi music is no more musicianly than "regenerate" art comes from "art in general."

What is found to be obliterated, stifled in music, is precisely what distinguishes it and what also figured in the heart of its interpretation that I will for convenience call "romantic": namely, an insurmountable and necessary—even desirable—*distance* between sound and sense, a distance without which sonority would cease to be what it is. Even by continuing to use a dated vocabulary, one would have to say that the "ineffable" does not constitute an oversignification, but, on the contrary, a beyond-significance [*outre-signifiance*] that it is not possible to enter and analyze under any kind of code (except under musical codes, which, precisely, are not semantic, not linguistic, and that are also not determinable as a "language of affects" in the proper sense of such an expression).

The intimacy of music is an intimacy more intimate than any evocation or any invocation. But for that very reason, it remains exactly at the distance of music from words, and that distance is not one that could separate a sovereign or sublime speech from a humble and subjugated speech. No speech lets itself be given form here, even if this form is intended as the form of the formless. Nazism had no other will than making the formless conform. But have this temptation, this fervor or this rage, left us? Can they leave us, so long as we have not restored to the *distance* from "meaning" all the extension and tension it requires?

How Music
Listens to Itself

*I*f someone listens to music without knowing anything about it—as we say of those who have no knowledge of musicology—without being capable of interpreting it, is it possible that he is actually listening to it, rather than being reduced to hearing [*entendre*] it? Or rather, if the term *entendre* [hear/understand] had to signify only a sonorous perception deprived of form, as soon as signals from everyday life are no longer perceived, is it possible that the listening can go beyond an immediate apprehension of emotional impulses, movements, and resonances confusedly dependent on acquired habits regarding rhythm and tonality (speed or slowness, major and minor modes . . .)? Without a doubt, musical listening allows one to link sensory apprehension to analysis of composition and execution, and by doing so, to justify the modulations of sensibility, from overall apprehension of a work to the detail of its moments or registers. Without a doubt, musical listening worthy of that name can consist only in a correct

combination of the two approaches or of the two dispositions, the compositional and the sensory.

The fact remains that the determination of the correct-
ness in question itself does not stem from any criteriology,
whether musicological or aesthetic. So all the questions
thus aroused continue to yield to scholarly and complex
investigations that leave an infinitely fragile but resistant
kernel of obscurity still intact: How are the musicianly
[*musicien*] and the musical shared or intermingled?

One has only to ask the question, however, to understand that it holds true not just for the subject of listening
but also for the subject of composition and execution. Musical science or technique does not by itself imply the most
profound, original, or convincing musicality. To be sure,
there are no examples—or almost none—of a naïve musician in the sense of Douanier Rousseau (although his "naï-
veté" is far from being devoid of technical sophistication
and savoir-faire), but there are many examples of talented
technicians whose musical faculty doesn't get beyond tepid
academic compositions.

It is even possible that this question of the interlinking
of the musicianly and the musical is the same question as
that of the sharing between a technical apprehension and
a sensory apprehension in all the realms of art: painting,
dance, architecture, or cinema. Actually, this time it is a
matter—according to very different modalities—of the
distance between what links a work to its means, conditions, and regulated contexts, and what makes it exist as

such, in its indivisible unity (which is, moreover, nothing but the indivisible unity of a whole and of the discrete units, all just as indivisible, of its parts, moments, components, aspects . . .).

What makes the work is nothing but this: what makes it in its totality and as its "whole" is present nowhere but in its parts or elements. Responsiveness to the work, likewise, is distributed over all the parts while remaining undivided within each part, each modality, and each passage of the work. What we are calling "work" is much less the completed production than this very movement, which does not "produce" but opens and continually holds the work open—or, more precisely, maintains the work as this opening that it essentially is, all the way to its conclusion, even if this conclusion takes shape from what music calls resolution.

To listen, as well as to look or to contemplate, is to touch the work in each part—or else to be touched by it, which comes to the same thing. There is probably no major difference between the musicianly/musical pair and the iconological/pictorial pair—if it is possible to use the terms this way—or the pair (same remark) of poetics/poetry or else all the pairs one can define for each aesthetic system. Each time it can only be a matter of a close combination of analysis and touch, each one sharpening or strengthening the other. An intimate and delicate marriage between sensation (or feeling, it's all the same) and the composition of the sensory.

What distinguishes music, however, is that composition, in itself, and the procedures of joining together never stop anticipating their own development and keep us waiting in some way for the result—or outcome—of their order, their calculations, their (musico)logic. Whether or not he is a musician, for someone who listens, the very instant a sonority, a cadence, a phrase touches him (of which he can, if he is a musician, determine the value, measure, etc.), he is propelled into an expectation, urged towards a presentiment. Whereas painting, dance, or cinema always retain in a certain present—even if it is fleeting—the movement and opening that form their soul (their sense, their truth), music, by contrast, never stops exposing the present to the imminence of a deferred presence, one that is more "to come" [*à venir*] than any "future" [*avenir*]. A presence that is not future, but merely promised, merely present because of its announcement, its prophecy in the instant.

Prophecy in the instant and *of* the instant: announcement in that instant of its destination outside of time, in an eternity. At every instant music promises its development only in order the better to hold and open the instant—the note, the sustaining, the beat—outside of development, in a singular coincidence of movement and suspense. It is a question of a hope: not a hope that promises itself possible futures, but rather an expectation that, without expecting anything, lets a touch of eternity come and come again. This owes everything and nothing to succession, to the incorporation of movement already past, or to the anticipation of its pursuit. Rather, each time it repeats the same beginning: the opening, the attack of sound, the one by which modulated sound is already preceded and succeeded without its zero point ever being able to be fixed in place. That is what sound resounds in: it demands itself again in order to be what it is: sonorous.

Music is the art of the hope for resonance: a sense that does not make sense except because of its resounding in itself. It calls to itself and recalls itself, reminding itself and by itself, each time, of the birth of music, that is to say, the opening of a world in resonance, a world taken away from the arrangements of objects and subjects, brought back to its own amplitude and making sense or else having its truth only in the affirmation that modulates this amplitude.

It is not a hearer [*auditeur*], then, who listens, and it matters little whether or not he is musical. Listening is musical when it is music that listens to itself. It returns to itself, it reminds itself of itself, and it feels itself as resonance itself: a relationship to self deprived, stripped of all egoism and all ipseity. Not "itself," or the other, or identity, or difference, but alteration and variation, the modulation of the present that changes it in expectation of its own eternity, always imminent and always deferred, since it is not in any time. Music is the art of making the outside of time return to every time, making return to every moment the beginning that listens to itself beginning and beginning again. In resonance the inexhaustible return of eternity is played—and listened to.

Notes

Listening

1. The word here is *entente*, meaning "agreement, understanding," from *entendre*, "to hear, to understand." Nancy is drawing a contrast between *écoute*, "listening," and *entente*.—Trans.

2. The verb here is *entend*, which can mean both "hears" and "understands."—Trans.

3. The origin of *–culto* is unknown; its intensive or frequentative quality, incidentally, is well vouched for.

4. As if the expression were taken from observing certain animals, like rabbits and many others, always listening and "on the lookout" . . .

5. This is characteristic of certain Latin languages. *Intendere* is Latin for "tend toward." The first use in French was in the sense of *tendre l'oreille* ["stretching the ear," listening]: although, in *écouter*, the ear goes toward the tension, in *entendre*, the tension wins over the ear. Moreover, it would be worthwhile to examine other associations in other languages: the Greek *akouī*, with the meanings of "understanding," "following," or "obeying"; the German *hören*, which gives us *hörchen*, "to obey"; the English *to hear*, in the sense of "to learn," "to be informed of," etc.

6. Tension that, without any doubt, is in relation to the "intension" that François Nicolas speaks of in "Quand l'oeuvre écoute la musique," in Peter Szendy, ed., *L'écoute* (Paris: Ircam/L'Harmattan, 2000), where

the first version of the present essay was published: between the two texts, there is more than just correspondence, a remarkable counterpoint.

7. Perhaps we are permitted to consider two positions or two destinations of music (whether it's the same music or two different genres): music heard and music listened to (or, as they used to be called, background music and concert music). The analogy would be difficult to make in the domain of the plastic arts (except perhaps with decorative painting).

8. Charles Rosen, *The Frontiers of Meaning: Three Informal Lectures on Music* (New York: Hill and Wang, 1994).

9. Indeed, the same is true, formally, for the visible: to understand a piece of music or a painting is to admit or recognize the uniquely pictorial or uniquely musical meaning; at least it's to *strain* toward such a uniqueness or toward its inaccessibility, toward the characteristic of the inappropriable. The difference is still there, and it is not merely an extrinsic difference of "media": it is a difference of meaning and in meaning (and we should deploy it for all perceptible registers). What confers a particular distinction on the sonorous and the musical (without its becoming a privilege) can only emerge little by little, and no doubt with difficulty . . . although nothing is clearer to us, or more immediately perceptible.

10. We'll risk saying: because of the considerable difference in speeds (or, for Einstein, in the limited nature of the speed of light), while sound spreads, light is instantaneous: the result of this is a quality of presence of the visual distinct from the coming-and-going quality unique to the sonorous.

11. Which is always at once the body that resounds and my body as a listener where that resounds, or that resounds with it.

12. That, in fact, is the perceptible condition in general: sounding operates as "gleaming" or "smelling" in the sense of emitting a smell, or else as the "palpating" of touching (palpating, palpitating—*palper, palpiter*: a small, repeated movement). Each sense is both an example and a differencing in such a "vibrating (itself)," and all senses vibrate among themselves, some against others and some with others, including the sense of meaning [*sens sensé*] . . . Which we still have to . . . understand. (How many, incidentally, senses there are, or whether they are

actually uncountable, is another question.) But, at the same time, we still have to discern how each perceptible system makes a different model and resonance for all the others . . . We'll note here for the moment how much sonorous amplification and resonance play a determining role (which it may not be possible to transpose exactly onto the visual plane) in the formation of music and of its instruments, as André Schaeffner points out in his *Origine des instruments de musique* (Paris: Mouton, 1968; 2d ed., Paris, École des hautes études en sciences sociales, 1994; I thank Peter Szendy, who helped me find this work): "In every case [treatment of the voice or fabrication of instruments by amplification or alteration of sounds] it is much less a question of 'imitating' than of surpassing something—the already known, the ordinary, the relatively moderate, the natural. Hence the extraordinary inventions, a propensity for acoustic monstrosities that would perplex physicists" (25).

13. Once it is agreed that touching gives the general structure or fundamental note of self-sensing [*se-sentir*]: in a way, every sense touches itself by sensing (and touches the other senses). At the same time, every perceptible mode or register exposes one of the aspects of "touching (itself)," separation or conjunction, presence or absence, penetration or retraction, etc. The "singular plural" structure and dynamics of all the senses, their way of being precisely "together" and touching themselves while still distinguishing themselves, would be the subject of another study. Here, I am only asking that we never lose sight of the fact that nothing is said of the sonorous that must not also be true "for" the other registers as well as "against" them, "next to" as well as in opposition, in a complementarity and in an incompatibility that are inextricable from each other as well as from the very meaning of perceived sense [*sens sensé*] . . . (This text was written and published in its first version before Jacques Derrida published *Le toucher, Jean-Luc Nancy* [Paris: Galilée, 2000], translated as *On Touching: Jean-Luc Nancy*, trans. Christine Irizarry [Stanford: Stanford University Press, 2005].)

14. *Espaces acoustiques* is the title of a composition by Gérard Grisey, who explores the realms of sonorities and their amplifications or intensifications.

15. *Se sentir*, a reflexive verb, literally "to feel oneself," means "to feel, to sense." English has no equivalent for the reflexive form of this verb.—Trans.

16. The pun here is on the word *accès*, "access, approach," which in a phrase like *un accès de colère* means "a fit of anger," or in *un accès de tristesse*, a wave of sadness. Nancy is contrasting *un accès au soi* ("an approach to the self") with *un accès de soi*, translated here as "a fit of self."—Trans.

17. "Echo of the subject": first resonance of a title by Philippe Lacoue-Labarthe to which I will refer later on.

18. This is the not the exclusive characteristic of the word *guet* (whose origin is in the direction of awakening, vigilance), but it is revealing that it is linked to surveillance more spontaneously in a culture where recognition of forms dominates . . .

19. Among a hundred different possible distributions and combinations of the "senses," I can, for my argument, outline this one: the visual (and the gustative) in relationship to *presence*, the auditory (and olfactory) in relationship to the *sign* (and the tactile beyond them both). Or else, two Greek examples of brilliance or glory: the visual, *doxa*, appearance in keeping with an expectation; and the acoustic, *kleos*, renown spread by word. But in this way, we will in any case have said nothing about the other senses (movement, tension, time, magnetism . . .).

20. Michelle Grangaud, *État civil* (Paris: P.O.L., 1999).

21. Pascale Criton, interview with Omer Corlaix, in *Pascale Criton: Les univers microtempérés* (Champigny-sur-Marne: Ensemble 2e2m, 1999), 26. On the mimetic comprehension of music and its issues, see Philippe Lacoue-Labarthe, "L'écho du sujet," to which I will have other occasions to refer (Philippe Lacoue-Labarthe, *Le sujet de la philosophie* [Paris: Aubier-Flammarion, 1979]; *Typography: Mimesis, Philosophy, Politics*, ed. Christopher Fynsk, introd. Jacques Derrida [1989; rpt. Stanford: Stanford University Press, 1998]). In fact, I am pursuing here what the declared intention of that text was: to penetrate just a little the "overwhelming power" (294 in the French, 203 in the English) of music, or to go back to the "ante-musical," where "the self / detects the sound of a voice that doubles its own," in the words of Wallace Stevens (from "The Woman That Had More Babies than That," *Opus Posthumous*) with which this text ends. I am concerned only with the resonance of such a voice, prolonging its reverberation into the thinking of Lacoue-Labarthe (isn't his name already echoing itself? La . . . La . . . : he hears me, he understands me . . .).

22. In speaking of "presence to self," one obviously places oneself where Jacques Derrida located the heart of his undertaking, principally starting from *La voix et le phénomène* (Paris: Presses Universitaires de France, 1967; translated as *Speech and Phenomena*, trans. and introd. David B. Allison [Evanston, Ill: Northwestern University Press, 1973]). In fact, one could reopen here the whole *chantier* ["construction site": there is a play on words here, since the word *chant*, or "song," is contained in *chantier*—Trans.] of this "voice": demonstrating that its sonority and its musicality come back to making *différance* "itself" resonate differently. But one should also quite simply remark that the philosophical privilege accorded by Husserl, after many others, to the silent resonance of a voice, as subject of the subject himself, is certainly not foreign (even by reversal) to the singular quality of sonorous penetration and emotion. A little further on, I will return, in the company of Granel, to the analysis of the "living present" of the presence-to-self.

23. Hearing and the sonorous do not, however, win from this a privilege in the strict sense of the term, although they draw from it a remarkable particularity. In a sense—and this bears repeating—all perceptible registers make up this approach to "self" (which is also to say, to "sense"). But the fact that they are many—and without any possible totalizing—marks this same approach, at once, of an internal diffraction, which perhaps in turn lets itself be analyzed in terms of repeats [*renvois*], echos, resonances, and also rhythms. One would have to prolong this analysis elsewhere, which also branches out, as we see, to an analysis of the plurality of the arts (cf. Jean-Luc Nancy, *Les muses* [Paris: Galilée, new enlarged edition, 2001], esp. "Les arts se font les uns contre les autres").

24. For it is suitable to reserve the possibility, demanded by Heidegger, of a transitivity of the verb *to be*.

25. Cf. esp. Erwin Strauss, *Le sens des sens*, trans. G. Thines and J.-P. Legrand (Grenoble: Jérôme Millon, 1989), 602 ff.

26. Cf. "Musique" in Jean-Luc Nancy, *Le sens du monde* (Paris: Galiée, 1993), 135.

27. Despite proximities, it would not be possible to apply completely such a description to the other modes of perceptible penetration, which are smell and taste, and even less to luminous penetration.

28. Act 1, scene 1, Gurnemanz, "Du siehst, mein Sohn, / zum Raum wird hier die Zeit [You see, my son, / here time becomes space]," when the scene shifts from outside the forest to inside the Grail Hall, with a great orchestral swell in which the major themes of the work return.

29. Cf. Strauss, *Le sens des sens*. See also, in the paper by Michel Chion that I heard at the Ircam conference, the themes of the impossibility of a *recoil* or a *coming closer* of the sonorous subject, as opposed to the visible subject, or the impossibility of an *overall view* as soon as the sonorous subject has lasted a certain amount of time.

30. In these exact words, by Pascal Quignard, *La haine de la musique* (Paris: Calmann-Lévy, 1996), 107.

31. Paul Valéry, *Cahiers II* (Paris: Gallimard, 1974), 974.

32. Ibid., 68.

33. Or, to insist again on the singular community of "senses": the "sonorous" dimension is the dimension of the dynamics of a come-and-go, manifest also, but differently, in visual or tactile intensity—the "visual" dimension would be that of the obviousness of the aspect or form; the "tactile" dimension, that of the impression of the texture, each manifesting just as much, but differently, in a certain intensity or modality of the others.

34. One can support this rhythmic constitution of the "self" more precisely with Nicolas Abraham, *Rythmes* (Paris: Flammarion, 1999; translated as *Rhythms: On the Work, Translation, and Psychoanalysis*, trans. Benjamin Thigpen and Nicholas T. Rand [Stanford: Stanford University Press, 1995]).

35. Cf. the analyses of primary retention and of the Kantian "I" that Bernard Stiegler carries out in *La technique et le temps, 3: Le temps du cinéma et la question du mal-être* (Paris: Galilée, 2001).

36. Remark made by the conductor Sergiu Celibidache, heard on the radio (October 1999). Unless one should also turn this statement around to say that there is no physical time, even the most carefully measured, that is not already cadence and even timbre, if the former is strictly monotone and the latter simple rustling of silence: the singular perceptible logic of *tick-tock* is that the identical sound, without the colorful variation of the *i* to the *o* in this onomatopoeia, differs, however, from itself, or differs its identity.

37. Gérard Granel, *Le sens du temps et de la perception chez E. Husserl* (Paris: Gallimard, 1968).

38. Of course, we could, and we should, also linger over the selection of the melody, separated from other sonorous and musical values (harmony, timbre, intensity).

39. Granel, *Le sens du temps et de la perception chez E. Husserl*, 118.

40. See above, n. 24.

41. How can one avoid noting that the etymology of *sonare*, in a semantic group of sound or noise, cannot be separated from another onomatopoeic group (where sound gives sense . . .) of which *susurrus* ("humming, murmuring") is the first representative (an "expressive word," Ernout and Meillet write, in which "the repetition and gemination of the 'r' are two characteristic traits"; *Dictionnaire étymologique de la langue latine* [Paris: Klincksieck, 1994], 670). And how can one not add that the word *mot* ("word") itself comes from *mutum*, which designates a sound deprived of sense, the *murmuring* emitted by repeating the syllable *mu*? (And for the Greek *sigī*, "silence," it is also sometimes suggested that it started with an "expressive syllable *si-*," as in *sitta*, which is a shepherd's call . . .). If the silent difference withdraws within music, doesn't sound deprived of sense withdraw into the heart (but not *from* the heart) of speech that is supposed to be meaningful? Music is not the origin of language, as people have so often wanted to think, but what withdraws and sinks into it.

42. In Plato's cave, there is more than just the shadows of objects being moved about outside: there is also the echo of the voices of those who move them, a detail we usually forget, since it is so quickly set aside by Plato himself in favor of the visual and luminous scheme exclusively.

43. For allophones: *sonner*, "to sound," can mean, in slang, "deafen," "knock out," and also "summon with a bell," as one used to do a domestic; on the other hand, *sonner* had, in old French, the sense of "playing" (a musical instrument) and "pronouncing" (a word), as well as "reciting a poem" (in an accentuated, loud way) or even "signifying, making a sense understood," before limiting its meaning, as today, to "making a sound," "reverberating," "resounding."

44. Cf. Giorgio Agamben, "La recherche de la voix dans le language, c'est cela la pensée," *La fine del pensiero*, *Le Nouveau Commerce*, nos. 53–54 (Paris, 1982).

Interlude

NOTE: The first part of this text was written for a *livre d'artiste* by Susanna Fritscher, entitled *Mmmmmmm* (Paris: Éditions au Figuré, 2000). The second part was added for its publication as a contribution to "Derrida lecteur," ed. Ginette Michaux and Georges Leroux, special issue, *Études françaises* 38. nos. 1–2 (2001).

1. I will keep relentlessly repeating: every "sense" plays this role, in its turn and at the same time . . .

2. But *moriendo* is not finishing; it is unfinishing [*infinissant*]. I am also thinking, of course, of the book to which Roger Laporte gave that title [*Moriendo*], but also of *mourir* [dying] as Blanchot means it, that is as *écrire*, writing, which also designates speech (the sense of sound) as infinite resonance (the sound of sense).

3. Bernard Baas, *De la chose à l'object* (Louvain: Peeters; Paris: Vrin, 1999), 149 ff.

4. Hence, in a sense, the "saying [*le dire*]," but the "saying" as non-said [*non-dit*] *and also* as non-saying [*non-disant*]: noisy, noise-making [*bruyant, bruissant*] . . . (Moreover, the pair of "saying" and "said" would lead us necessarily to encounter a well-known theme of Levinas, which he mingles with the theme of the "voice of silence" (e.g., in *Autrement qu'être ou au-delà de l'essence* [The Hague: Martinus Nijhoff, 1978], 172; *Otherwise than Being, or Beyond Essence*, trans. Alphonso Lingis [The Hague: Martinus Nijhoff, 1981], 135). The question of the relationships, in Levinas, between vision, hearing, and touch merits study (cf. Edith Wyschogrod, "Doing before Hearing: On the Primacy of Touch," in *Textes pour Emmanuel Lévinas* [Paris: Jean-Michel Place, 1980]). Encountering a whole ordering of a perceptible system (in all the senses of *sense*, including the "sense" of acting) would undoubtedly be a remarkable case of complications and limits: the perceptible can be approached only by its plural singularity, the only way it "makes sense."

5. Baas, *De la chose à l'object*, 197.

6. Ibid., 217–218.

7. Not, once again, that this reverberation is absent from other perceptible systems: on the contrary, it comprises them all (a color or a

texture also "resounds," one might say). But sonority, ultimately, is *nothing but* its reverberation: as if it didn't pose, deposit, a consistent quality like color or texture; thus we have recourse to the names of these qualities to speak of the sonorous (of its color or its texture, among a hundred other metaphors). It is perhaps in this sense that we should understand Schelling when he writes that if all art is a penetration of the divine word into the finitude of the world, in plastic arts the word presents itself petrified, whereas in music "the living having entered death—the word pronounced within the finite—is still perceptible as sound [*Klang*, or 'resonance']" (*Philosophie der Kunst*, §73). For Schelling, however, that is not yet the summit of art, which can only be in language, where the word remains infinitely uttered, though it is privileged in the sonorous element, since it is thanks to that element that there can be effectuated in the world the divine word's act of affirmation (if I can thus reduce the considerations that end the *Philosophy of Art* as we have it). Impossible not to notice the circle: starting from the motif of the "word" God is designated as originally speaking, which confers on speech (very precisely distinguished by Schelling from a possible language of gesture) the entirely natural, if I may say so, privilege of being its echo, resonance of the original pure sonority, and hence resonance of a resonance of/in origin. A circle of sense and sound is posed in the beginning, and no doubt an era is marked by that until our own, through musical romanticism, and Schopenhauer, then Nietzsche. If I pause briefly to point this out, it is because it should be very clear that the whole analysis I am suggesting, with the characteristics I borrow from Granel, Lacoue-Labarthe, Baas, and Lacan, *at every instant risks not being distinguished from this typically metaphysical circle, which* produces nothing less than the resolution of presence to self at the same time as that of the sensibility of the intelligible and of the intelligibility of the perceptible. (A similar figure of a circle can be found in Hegel: "The ear, without physically turning itself toward objects, perceives the result of this inner trembling of the body by which is manifested . . . a first ideality coming from the soul" ["La musique," Introduction, *Esthéthique*, trans. S. Jankélévitch (Paris: Flammarion, 1979), 4:322; trans. J.-P. Levèvre and V. von Schenk (Paris: Aubier, 1997), 3:122; the latter has a mistake in this sentence.]) In fact, here we are exactly at the point where, simultaneously, a twofold tension of presence is in play, which, in order to be *to* self, emerges endlessly *from* self, along with another twofold tension of the empirical and of the transcendental, an experience of the senses dependent on an ontotheological postulation, which in turn depends on perceptible stances, and also a twofold tension of mimesis, with sound being the image of sense as much as sense is the echo of sound . . . at the very least to enunciate the thing in the lexicon of these determinations and their oppositions. I am not trying to evade or to raise all these ambivalences: I am content with making them heard [*entendre*, understood].

8. Baas speaks of this himself (incidentally, he is a musician as well as a philosopher). He does so, however, by quoting Lévi-Strauss, who makes music dependent on language, saying in a somewhat Schelling-like way that music is "language minus sense" (*De la chose à l'object*, 196). I would argue, not conversely but in parallel, that this utterance must be made to resound in a different way: "music is sense minus language." But perhaps, in the end, "sense" does not have the same sense in both cases—and sense in general is what it is only when distanced from self. To go back to a hypothetical *etymon* of "sense," don't we evoke a family of terms around the idea of traversing, traveling? (But traveling isn't necessarily "striving toward": it can signify "walking," wandering; to visit [*visiter*] is not to aim at [*viser*] . . .)

9. Or what Marie-Louise Mallet calls "the night of the philosopher" and analyzes in her essential book, *La musique en respect* (Paris: Galilée, 2002).

10. According to Artaud's phrase, often repeated by Deleuze: body not organized toward a purpose or function, a "de-territorialized" body, body-potency [*corps-puissance*] and not body-instrument (or else musical instrument . . . : which would lead us to wonder if musical instruments are actually "instruments" and not really amplified bodies instead, excrescent, resonant).

11. Which also implies surmounting, outsmarting [*déjouer*], or displacing the "impossibility of circumscribing the essence of listening" to a *theoretical* system, if the latter has already referred the audible and the visible back to each other, by echo or by reflection, or by an eidetic reflection of the echo (cf. the whole analysis of Reik by Lacoue-Labarthe,

"L'écho du sujet," in *Le sujet de la philosophie* [Paris: Aubier-Flamma-rion, 1979], 247–50; *Typography: Mimesis, Philosophy, Politics*, ed. Chris-topher Fynsk, introd. Jacques Derrida [1989; rpt. Stanford: Stanford University Press, 1998], 163–65). Thus we find ourselves at the point of extreme ambivalence between sense and sound, as between theory (or speculation) and listening (or repercussion). Lacoue-Labarthe writes: "It is . . . in the specular reduction [of listening] that the question of style is decided (or lost)" (ibid., 251 in the French, 166 in the English). It is, in fact, a question of music as of the *style* by which the acoustic is valid as such, and not in a specular reduction (which is valid by turns and all together for all the registers of sense).

12. France Arte and the Institut national de l'audiovisuel [National Television Archive].

13. One can find the equivalent, as I am not unaware, in any dis-course on painting, especially one intended for children (the painter tells a story; a shape or a color conveys an emotion, etc.). The thing is, how-ever, less emphasized and, moreover, recourse to formal commentary (composition, mass, relationships, etc.) is directly more practicable, at least in a schematic way, with painting than with music. We'll put it simply: it does not require the same technicality. Yet the distance be-tween technico-musicological discourse and "interpretive" discourse is often not only vast but even veers toward mutual opposition and exclu-sion. We really ought to linger for some time on this question elsewhere. There is nothing empirical or fortuitous about it, contrary to what some people think. Musical technique is not of the same order as techniques in the plastic arts: the latter are subordinated to a presentation in which they disappear; the former remains somehow autonomous, as much in a separate state (writing, analysis, order of calculations of all kinds, in-cluding the making of stringed instruments) as in the state incorporated in the performance. There must be some kind of correspondence here with the vibratory and syncopated (in every sense) property of music: that relative autonomy or that technical distance emphasizes the singu-lar autonomy of a "sense/sound" pair that can only be detached from each other in relation to an order of "interpretation" and that place it in a greater difficulty than the one in which a plastic presentation places it, whose relatively more "object-oriented" stance lets a mode of deci-pherment or hermeneutics operate on it more readily. That said, there

is *also* the result of a question asked of the "hermeneutics" of art itself: How can it ensure the capture of a "sense" that is not at all a "sensed" sense given or lent by it to art, but the sense *of* art *to* art itself? (Cf., on this subject, Jean-Luc Nancy, "Autrement dire," *Po&sie*, no. 89 [Paris: Belin, 1999].)

14. The references ought to be more numerous here than I can make them. Of course, to more than one text by Adorno, but also to texts by Michel Butor, Pierre Schaeffer, Charles Rosen, André Boucourechliev, Peter Szendy, Marie-Louise Mallet, Martha Grabocz, Michael Levinas, Danielle Cohen-Levinas, etc. Rather than a few scattered references, I will limit myself to this allusion: the question demands a separate treatment.

15. Which will have engendered, especially since the development of instrumental music independent of voice and dance, and even more since romanticism, a certain type of titling, unknown till then, forming in and of itself a kind of hermeneutic program, hence also a programming for listening—for which the title of the Piano Sonata No. 23 by Beethoven, the *Appassionata* (a feminization of a term used as indication of movement), could constitute the symbol. The question of affect should be treated by itself: the question of an "imitation" or of a "production" of affects (*mimesis* and/or *methexis*), the question of what the Greeks called *ethos* in music (disposition of the body, temperament, character with which a *melos*, a precise musical assembling, agrees in a predetermined way—a "melodic structure that, for the Greeks, is *identical* to the 'how-one-feels' that for us it *expresses*," as Johannes Lohmann puts it in *Mousiké et Logos: Contributions à la philosophie et à la théorie musicale grecques*, trans. Pascal David [Mauvezin: TER, 1989], 20), the question of codes by which a relationship between affect and determined musicality is established and, of course, the question of knowing if affect is a signified, or a sense like any other.

16. Pierre Schaeffer, "Du cadre au coeur du sujet," in *Psychanalyse et musique*, ed. Jacques and Anne Caïn (Paris: Les Belles Lettres, 1982), 79 (sent to me by Peter Szendy). One can also refer to the "multiple" "Oh's!" and "Ah's!" of music mentioned by Marie-Louise Mallet under

the emblematic title "Un récit sans récit," in *Rue Descartes*, no. 21, *Musique, affects et narrativité*, ed. Danielle Cohen-Levinas (Paris: Presses Universitaires de France, 1998).

17. Benveniste demonstrated this perfectly in an article on music and language published in two issues of *Semiotica*, of which I confess I have only a memory and no concrete reference (it appeared in the 1960s).

18. It is remarkable that we can find, in the etymology of the word *phonī*, a contest between a derivation from the visible (via *phemi*, "to speak," but above all "to expose," "to bring to light," "to say") and another from the sonorous (via the root **gwen*, "to resound").

19. Francis Ponge, "Méthodes," in *Le grand recueil* (Paris: Gallimard, 1961), 220–21. Ponge continues: "Does that mean—because I say that each text carries its speaking at the very instant it is conceived— that each text carries nothing but speaking? Certainly not." We could add that this diction is corollary to a certain interruption (suspension, syncope) of the discursive continuity of sense, of which we have a pronounced form in the fragment as characterized by Roland Barthes: "The fragment has its ideal: a high condensation, not of thought, or of wisdom, or of truth (as in the Maxim), but of music: 'development' is contrasted with 'tone,' something articulated and sung, a diction: there is where *timbre* should reign. Webern's 'Short Pieces': no cadence: what sovereignty he places in *coming to an abrupt end*!" (*Roland Barthes par Roland Barthes* [Paris: Seuil, 1975], 98).

20. *Dicere* is first of all "to show" (e.g., *indicare*); the frequentative *dictare* implies, with repetition and insistence, "saying in a loud voice": as if the sonorous were an intensification of seeing, a placing in tension of presence.

21. How can we listen, in the West, when the great tonal system is undone, and when "in the era of contemporary music, there is an essential dissociation of writing and perception . . . [an] abyss that henceforth radically separates the eye from the ear," as François Nicolas says, quoted by Sofia Cascalho in a study devoted to this question (*La liberté s'entend*, a doctoral dissertation in music directed by Antoine Bonnet, Université de Paris VIII, September 1999, 9)? This also means that the

contemporary era of music, bringing about the dissolution of a coded and signifying ensemble, *makes us listen or restores us to listening*—and, precisely, listening to all musical registers, not only those of Western musical provenance.

22. Which happens to art as a whole in what we call, often in a rather confused way, "the end of representation." As for the demonstration of rhythm and timbre in the musical aspect of this mutation or deconstruction of art by itself, I would be quite incapable of giving either a musicological or historical analysis of it. I refer only, and tacitly, to the studies by François Nicolas and Antoine Bonnet, by Jean-Claude Risset, to others by Michael Levinas or by Philippe Manoury, by Peter Szendy or by Pascale Criton, but without claiming any exhaustiveness or theoretical mastery, since I really have everything still to learn. I am taking the risk of an uninitiated discourse. Yet I am trying not to speak of anything but what a contemporary ear gathers, if only it strains toward sonorities transformed by a considerable number of factors, which go from the new rhythmic significances coming from so many kinds of popular music up to the synthesis of sounds by computer, including all the techniques of sound processing (*sampling*, *remix*, etc.). Concerning this also, and whatever the importance is of techniques of synthesis on the order of images, attention is drawn to a discrepancy between the sonorous and the visual: the mutation of images preserves a general characteristic that I would call, to exaggerate a little, a "picture," whereas sonorous mutation opens up and hollows out in us and around us new caves where the "musical" loses its "face," in brief (but the pictorial also loses it in performance, for example). Moreover, a special exploration would be necessary of the sonorous world of the cinema and of video, in the way that the acoustic and the optical mutually affect each other.

23. We must remember, without lingering over this, to what point the foregrounding of the rhythm and timbre pair, in musical thought and practice today, is linked to the deconstruction of the musical system(s) of the West (tuning that is stricter because of polyphony, the examples of "consonance," the fixed values of notes and the exclusion of other sounds, that is, other frequencies, etc.). There has resulted from this an opening up of listening to other kinds of music, the creation of

new instruments, the implementation of sonorous resources that are "ill-tempered" according to traditional norms, and a considerable modification of our stances toward and our capacities for listening.

24. And pro-clamation, re-clamation . . . : the whole family of clamor, a word stemming from a root that is also "expressive" of a noise or cry . . .

25. An obvious allusion to a well-known theme of Freud's (especially in the essay *Die Verneinung* ["Negation"]).

26. On the themes of outside and inside, of envelopment, see the studies carried out by François Zourabichvili in his seminar at the Collège international de philosophie.

27. In the sense that Lacoue-Labarthe uses it: fixing, freezing a type or a model.

28. Lacoue-Labarthe, "L'écho du sujet," *Le sujet de la philosophie*, 291; *Typography*, 201.

29. Cf. the main conclusions elaborated by Pierre-Sauvanet in *Le rythme grec d'Héraclite à Aristote* (Paris: Presses Universitaires de France, 1999).

30. Antoine Bonnet, "La part de l'insaisissable," in *Le timbre, une métaphore pour la composition* (Paris: Bourgois, 1991), 351; and "Conditions et possibilités actuelles de la composition musicale," doctoral thesis, Paris, École normale supérieure, 1991.

31. Perhaps, therefore, one never utters anything but the primordial condition of a "phenomenological intentionality" that is thought without any reservations: but in another vocabulary and in a different tone.

32. Cf. the same studies by Antoine Bonnet.

33. Ludwig Wittgenstein, "Notes sur l'expérience privée et les *sense data*," in *Philosophica II*, trans. Elizabeth Rigal (Mauvezin: TER, 1999), 7 and 15. It is interesting to find much earlier, in Lagneau: "Since it is not by a distinct act of mind that we compose the idea of timbre, it is perhaps not true to call it perception; perceiving timbre, we measure nothing. . . . Intensity and timbre are immediate sensations, in which we can note complexity only by using external analysis. There is something ultimate there for consciousness" (*Célèbres leçons et fragments* [Paris: Presses Universitaires de France, 1964], 200).

34. Cf. Emile Leipp, "Timbre," in the *Encyclopedia Universalis*, and the related articles.

35. "Pitch" [*hauteur*, literally "height"] is also a remarkable metaphor—insofar, of course, as one can still use here a logic of "metaphor" and "literal meaning". . .—whose relationship with space and with the mechanism of the body we should investigate (as in "low-pitched" and "high-pitched," *grave* and *aigu*).

36. More generally, we should examine those contagious referrals of timbre to the register of physical sounds (liquid, flow, rustling, banging, tearing), to that of animal voices (howling, growling, chirping, mooing), to that of materials (brassy, wooden), then to all the registers that the description of listening to instruments or voices seeks (what plucks or slides, what strikes, what vibrates) and even the spectacle of bodies in the postures of instrumentalists or singers (plucking, sliding, swelling out, releasing, striking, touching): there is a very impressive circulation of metaphors, metonymies, comparisons, identifications throughout all language about music and about sound in general (think about the words for sonority, even in French, to say nothing of German). Sonority does not inhabit language in quite the same way as the other perceptible qualities.

37. Note that this modern etymology was not known by the Greeks, who linked the word to *typto*, "to strike," and hence to the *typos* family: I would add to Lacoue-Labarthe's meditation this proximity between two strokes wherein one, with the tambourine, starts rhythm, whereas the other, with cold type, stops the dance and freezes the model . . .

38. Jacques Derrida, *Marges de la philosophie* (Paris: Minuit, 1972), xiii; *Margins of Philosophy*, trans. Alan Bass (Chicago: University of Chicago Press, 1982), xix.

Coda

1. In fact, three versions of the painting exist, as well as two others where the man is playing a lute. This repetition of the motif, so obstinately replayed by the painter, and the details of the scene, as well as

the general motif of music in painting (Vermeer and Picasso, Gentileschi and Klee, and all the "concerts" and all the "singers") obviously require further study, which I will undertake elsewhere.

"March in Spirit in Our Ranks"

NOTE: The title of this essay is a line from "Das Horst Wessel Lied," marching song of the S.A.: The summons is addressed to the dead victims "of the Red Front and the Reactionaries"; Horst Wessel was chosen as representative of those victims.

1. Cf. Philippe Lacoue-Labarthe and Jean-Luc Nancy, *Le mythe nazi* (La Tour d'Aigues: Éditions de l'Aube, 1998).

2. Quoted by Lionel Richard, *Le nazisme et la culture* (Brussels: Edition Complexe, 1988), 192.

Milton Keynes UK
Ingram Content Group UK Ltd.
UKHW020148081224
452180UK00001B/32